BRIGHT IDEAS

The Outdoor Classroom

D1380159

**Edited by Brian Keaney
and Bill Lucas**

Published by Scholastic Publications Ltd,
Villiers House, Clarendon Avenue,
Leamington Spa, Warwickshire CV32 5PR

© 1992 Scholastic Publications Ltd

Edited by Brian Keaney and Bill Lucas

Contributors: Christine Andrews; Krysia
Baczala; Karen Brock; Elaine Garfitt; Jane
Giles; Kathryn Humphries; Susan
Humphries; Brian Keaney; Rosemary
Keaney; Stash Kozlowski; Bill Lucas;
Catherine Mills; Susan Rowe; Heather
Swain; Gill Thomas; Wendy Titman
Sub-edited by Magdalena Hernas
Illustrated by Maureen Bradley
Front and back covers designed by
Anna Oliwa
Photograph by Martyn Chillmaid
Typeset by Typesetters (Birmingham) Ltd
Printed in Great Britain by Loxley Brothers
Ltd, Sheffield
Artwork by Steve Williams Design,
Leicester

**British Library Cataloguing in Publication
Data**
A catalogue record for this book is available from the
British Library.

ISBN 0 590 53034-8

Contents

Introduction

LEARNING THROUGH LANDSCAPES

The Learning Through Landscapes research project was set up in 1986 to investigate the design, use, management and development of school grounds throughout the United Kingdom. Four years and many hundreds of school visits later, this research was published by the Learning Through Landscapes Trust in the form of a detailed report, and by the Department of Education and Science as *The Outdoor Classroom*.

Both these publications documented what many teachers, parents and pupils have known for a long time: that most school grounds are completely unsuited to the needs of children. All too often, the project found grounds which were treeless, devoid of shelter or seating and, in a large number of cases, all-asphalt. Even those schools with more land frequently offered only closely-mown flat grass spaces as an alternative to tarmac.

Such empty spaces are extremely harmful to children. They offer little more than an area in which football can be played. Children, especially boys, tend to career around them at speed, and the accident books of many headteachers bear witness to the dangers of such activity.

More importantly, this type of landscape can undermine the best efforts of even the most dedicated staff in a variety of ways. Bored, wet, cold and unhappy children are hardly likely to be in a suitable frame of mind to start learning when they return to the classroom. Young people experiencing such an alien environment are unlikely to have any sense of pride in their school and its surroundings. They may well develop a pretty jaundiced view of the environment in general. Some may wonder about the attitudes of their teachers, who seem to put up with such an intolerable situation. They

cannot be expected to guess that staff may themselves be unhappy with the school grounds.

Learning Through Landscapes has reminded all those concerned with education of the extent of the problem.
- There are more than 70,000 hectares of land around schools in the United Kingdom alone.
- Children spend well over a quarter of their school time in the grounds.
- Far too many school grounds are all-asphalt.

The earth itself is often the material most readily to hand and yet most easily overlooked. By mounding and contouring the land, a school can individualise its site and produce the banks, hollows and microclimates necessary for environmental diversity. Most schools would benefit from perimeter and internal structure planting which gives a 'green' feel even to urban sites. Schools, like supermarkets and sports centres, are responsible for their impact on the immediate environment. Too often, the entry points to school sites are uniformly squalid or austere.

The Learning Through Landscapes Trust, set up in 1990, has shown how to change the design and use of school grounds all over the United Kingdom. Thousands of schools have begun to see the benefits of treating the land on their doorstep as an educational resource and not just a grey or green gap between the school and the road.

A LANDSCAPE FOR CHILDREN

Architects and landscape architects are sometimes criticised for designing for themselves rather than for those who will use what they have created. This is particularly true of schools and school grounds, whose design should reflect

children's educational, social and emotional needs. This means that the grounds need to offer:
● a choice of quality design and materials – schools benefit from elaborate detailing such as patterns of brick, pillars, arches, sculpture, steps, cornices, wrought-iron work;
● appropriate scale – not vast empty spaces, but smaller, more intimate areas within the grounds with which children can identify;
● seating – formal seating, low walls and mounds for children to sit and chat, places to hide, spots where huddles of several children can meet;
● shelter – a chance to escape from the wind, rain and adults;
● diversity – a wide range of equipment, habitats (including water), colours and shapes, markings, flora and fauna, to stimulate the widest possible variety of educational activities.

Above all, it is clear that, in order to ensure suitable and reasonably long-lasting changes, children must be closely involved in the process of any change. This is one of the most important lessons of community architecture and one that successful schools are taking very seriously. The act of improving the school landscape is itself an appropriate curriculum activity.

A HOLISTIC APPROACH

In most schools, grounds are used for play during breaks and for PE and games. Learning Through Landscapes believes that every aspect of school life can be enhanced by work in the grounds.

The formal curriculum
Public land should be used to inform people about environmental responsibility and this process should start at school. If teachers are willing to teach outside the classroom, this awareness will be encouraged. Every subject in the National Curriculum can be taught in the grounds, with particularly rich opportunities presenting themselves in maths, technology, science, geography, PE and art. Outdoor teaching is also relevant in the case of the cross-curricular themes of environmental education, personal and social education and citizenship.

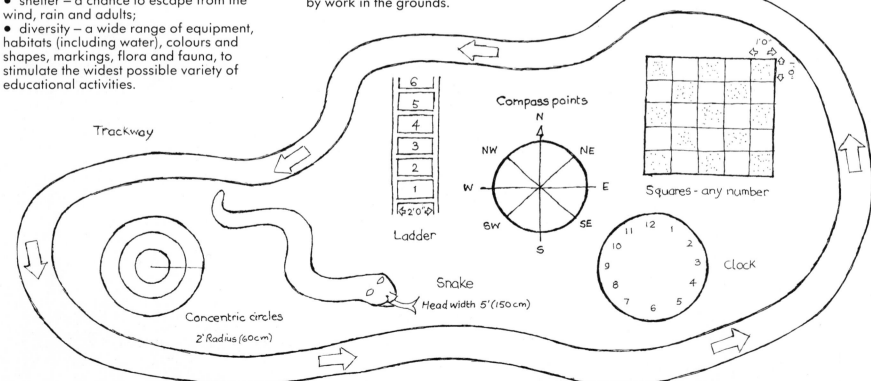

Trackway

Concentric circles

2' Radius (60cm)

Ladder

Snake

Head width 5' (150cm)

Compass points

N
NW   NE
W   E
SW   SE
S

Squares - any number

Clock

The informal curriculum
Formal teaching accounts for only about three-quarters of what children learn at school. Through play and other informal interactions, they constantly learn complex lessons about their own emotional and social development. The quality of the school environment has a great deal of influence on the children's behaviour. At worst, it can encourage bullying and other antisocial activities; at best, it can promote positive social behaviour and provide endless stimulation. School grounds which offer a variety of different areas, for example a place where board games and chanting games can be played, offer children the opportunity to pursue a full range of informal activities.

The hidden curriculum
Fencing, entrances, pathways, signposting, lighting, the quality of maintenance, all give powerful messages to both children and teachers. The manner in which the children are organised and spoken to on-site by teachers, lunchtime supervisors and other adults also contributes to the teaching environment. There are significant actions which schools can take to ensure positive outcomes in the vast majority of cases, actions which can help to develop a sense of ownership and pride in the school. The simple decision to have school meals outside on fine days can transform attitudes to this aspect of school life.

LOCAL FINANCING MANAGEMENT OF SCHOOLS

Like it or not, headteachers and their governing bodies nowadays need to become land managers. Money allocated for site maintenance can be used to improve the school grounds. Schools may decide to carry out the maintenance of their grounds in new and more imaginative ways, which may be of direct benefit to all aspects of the curriculum.

USING THIS BOOK

There are fifteen chapters in this book. The first eleven deal with the core and foundation subjects. They are described by subject only for ease of planning in a subject-based National Curriculum. Teachers unused to working outdoors will find the ideas in these chapters give them the opportunity to try out individual, self-contained activities. However, many ideas relate to more than one subject area and could, therefore, have been placed in more than one category.

Later in the book, two chapters present activities organised into cross-curricular themes of Celebrations and Journeys. In fact, we hope that much of what is taught will be part of a larger programme of study and that individual ideas will be grouped together to form longer-term schemes of work.

The penultimate chapter, 'Surveying the school grounds', fits very well into the technology curriculum, although it involves almost every other subject. It is followed by reproducible pages to be used during the survey.

The Resources page at the back offers at-a-glance information on grant schemes, useful publications and organisations.

Throughout, we assume that a methodology which places high emphasis on problem-solving, first-hand observation, data-handling and on a variety of other active learning skills, will be most suited to this kind of work.

English

A phonic scavenger hunt

Age range
Five to seven.

Group size
The whole class.

What you need
No special requirements.

What to do
This activity is designed to give children practice in phonic recognition.

Take the children for a walk around the school grounds. Ask them to name objects in the grounds which begin with the same sound, for example, for the s sound in 'snake', they might find snail, slug, sand, soil and snow. Older children can take clipboards, pencils and paper with them and write down the names of the objects they have seen or found.

Obviously sounds such as x or z will pose problems. You may want to plant appropriate objects or small cards with their images throughout the grounds.

Follow-up
● Make an alphabet of the grounds, each letter being represented by something found or seen there. The children could draw pictures to illustrate it. You might be able to involve parents with artistic skills and produce a compendium for the use of the whole school.
● The alphabet could also be sung or chanted. You might like to make it into a school rap!

A sensory walk

Age range
Five to eleven.

Group size
The whole class.

What you need
Bags, trays, egg-boxes and any other suitable collecting equipment.

What to do
Developing a sense of place is very important to all of us. What distinguishes a particular place from the rest of the environment is how we feel about it. This exercise will help the children tune into their feelings about the school grounds and express them in words.

Take the children for a walk around the grounds. Ask them to concentrate on their sensations. Can they feel the wind? Is it warm or cold? Can they see their breath in front of them when they breathe out? Stop at more than one point and ask the children to close their eyes and listen. What sounds do they hear? Other children in the school? Traffic? What can they smell? Flowers?

School dinner? Ask them to feel, with their eyes still closed, some of the surfaces around them: a brick wall, the bark of a tree, window panes. Ask them to look at the sky. What are the clouds like? What shapes do they make? What does the bark of the tree look like? Does it remind them of anything else?

Ask each child to bring back one or two objects from the walk, for example, leaves, conkers, twigs or stones. Back in the classroom, ask questions such as the following:
- Where did you go?
- What did you smell?
- What did you hear?
- What were you reminded of?
- Did anything strike you as strange or funny?

Ask the children to find words to describe their sensations and impressions. You might find it helpful to give them some words to start with, for example, round, hard, soft, colourful, squiggly, friendly, dangerous, modern, old-fashioned, crumbling, peeling, sooty, fresh. But be careful to let the children generate their own lists.

Write the word lists on large pieces of sugar paper or on the blackboard. This is a good way to show how adjectives are used. With older children, it can also lead to a discussion of how imagery describes one thing in terms of another – clouds like castles, bark like skin, for example.

Ask the children to think about other things which words on the list can describe. Suggest that the lists will be useful when the children come to write their descriptions of the walk.

Follow-up
Make a display of the objects the children have brought back. Mount it alongside the writing. You might also like to match this activity with 'Serial vision' on page 72.

The playground games book

Age range
Five to eleven.

Group size
Small groups.

What you need
Existing playground markings, chalk for marking new ones, paper, drawing materials, felt-tipped pens.

What to do
The purpose of this activity is to help the children create their own compendium of playground games.

Allow the children to use existing markings and dice or other small equipment to give a demonstration of the games they know. Ask each group to choose a game which they are going to explain to others. Tell them to agree on the rules and then explain the game to the rest of the class. Does the explanation make sense? Does it cover eveything?

Older children might like to bring in instructions for familiar games like draughts or Ludo. How are they set out? Are they easy to understand? What features (such as step-by-step numbering) are helpful?

The children might also try to make up their own games and to test them out, making new playground designs if necessary.

Finally, the older children will be ready to try writing out their games in the form of illustrated instructions. These could be incorporated into the Playground Games Book.

This activity provides an opportunity for older children to interview younger ones about the games they play.

Follow-up
● There are a number of published collections of children's games such as *Children's Games In Street And Playground* by Iona and Peter Opie, which may help in developing the playground games.
● You might also consider creating quiet corners in the playground by cordoning off areas with benches, planters or logs to give children somewhere to play board games, read or just socialise.

Hunting the beast

Age range
Five to eleven.

Group size
The whole class.

What you need
No special requirements.

What to do
Talk to the children about fabled creatures which people claim to have seen, such as the Loch Ness Monster or the Abominable Snowman. What are they said to be like? What sort of things do they do?

Ask the children to imagine that a strange creature has been seen in the school grounds. What might it look like? Would it resemble other known creatures? Who would have seen it and when?

Take the children for a walk in the grounds to decide where the creature would have its den. Discuss whether it would prefer a dry place or a wet one, what it would eat, whether it would leave any marks or traces.

When they have decided on the beast's habitat, talk about what it would do. Would it be frightened or frightening? Might it have special, perhaps magical, powers? Could it communicate or even talk? What would make it happy? What would make it angry?

Now ask the children to write about the creature. They might like to write a poem or a prose description of it. Older children could write a story of what happened to someone who met it.

Follow-up
Older children could interview witnesses and make a newspaper report about sightings of the creature.

Walking the bounds

Age range
Seven to eleven.

Group size
The whole class, small groups.

What you need
A collection of nature poems, dressing-up clothes, sugar paper, adhesive tape, sticks, pens.

What to do
Children are often asked to sit indoors and read nature poems. These can become much more enjoyable when read out of doors as part of a ceremony or a ritual. The old English custom of walking the bounds lends itself very well to this activity.

Explain to the children the meaning of the custom of 'walking' or 'beating' the parish bounds by striking certain points with rods at regular times during the year, for example, during the harvest or on the first day of spring. Ask the children to choose an occasion for walking the school bounds. Alternatively, choose a sunny day or an aftermath of a storm as your occasion.

Begin by reading out a selection of nature poems such as 'The North Wind Doth Blow' for younger children or 'The Months' by Christina Rosetti for the older ones. *A Year Full of Poems*, edited by Michael Harrison and Christopher Stuart-Clark (1991) Oxford University Press and other similar anthologies offer a variety of poems for different seasons and occasions. Make sure you include some unrhymed poetry so that the children do not feel that their own poems will have to rhyme.

Ask the children what it is that makes some types of writing, like lyrical poetry, particularly suitable for performing. Would a cooking recipe or a comic strip sound as good read out?

Take the children outside and ask them to feel the weather, to look at the sky, the trees, the grass underfoot. They should concentrate on their sensations and think of the best words to describe them. Back in the classroom, they can start writing their own poems focusing on their experience.

When they have finished writing, the children can prepare for reading their poems aloud, individually or together in groups. Group reading will require a rehearsal beforehand. Make sure each member of the group has a copy of the relevant poem.

In preparation for the ceremony, ask the children if they would like to wear special hats or robes. These could reflect traditional colour symbolism, for example, blue for the sky, yellow for the sun, green for spring. The children could use dressing-up clothes or make basic costumes from sugar paper. They will also need a stick for 'beating' the bounds.

Now ask the children to choose a number of specific points on the school boundaries to hold the ceremony and to agree which poems they will read out at which points. Take them out into the school grounds, making sure you conduct the ceremony with gravity and concentration.

When you reach the agreed spots in the grounds, the children should read out their poems as rehearsed in the classroom.

Follow-up

• Other such customs, still practised in parts of the British Isles, include clipping the church in Wickworth, Derbyshire, in which people link arms around their church on 8 September; bawming the thorn, in which people decorate a thorn tree with ribbons and flowers, practised in Appleton Thorn in Cheshire; and well dressing, known in many parts of Britain, in which wells and springs are decked with flowers. All of these can be adopted by schools as their annual rituals. The children may also like to find out about other such customs in Britain or abroad.

• You might like to contact Common Ground (see Resources, page 126), an organisation which has done much to revive local customs.

A guided tour

Age range
Nine to eleven.

Group size
Pairs.

What you need
Notepads and pens, a tape recorder.

What to do
Tell the children that they will be making guidebooks to help visitors look around the school. Ask them if they have ever visited a famous building, like the Tower of London or a National Trust property. If so, who took them around? If people were visting the school, what sort of things could be pointed out to them? Are there any good places for visitors to stop and look around?

Talk to the children about taking notes. You should explain that notes are not written out in full sentences. They serve as reminders, rather like a shopping list.

Take the whole class on a walk around the school grounds. Stop at regular intervals and talk with them about what they can see. You might ask questions such as the following:

- Why do you think this is a good place to stop?
- What is the view like from here?
- What noises can you hear?
- What can you smell?
- What is this part of the building used for?
- When do you think it was built?
- What sort of tree is this?

Ask them to make notes at each point.

Now send them off in pairs along the same route. This time ask them to take turns giving each other a guided tour of the grounds, using the notes to help them. You might find it helpful to start with some trust and leadership games, like the ones described on page 179.

When they have practised their guided tours, each pair could take the whole class around a part of the grounds. Afterwards, the children could discuss the tour. How successful was it? They could return to the best places and make some drawings or take photographs.

Now they are ready to begin to make a class guidebook. It might help to have some copies of published guides for them to look at. They should write down their comments about each of the stopping-off places and paste in the photographs or drawings.

Follow-up

● The children might like to invite parents into the school and take them on a guided tour.
● You could arrange to share the work with another local school or schools and produce a joint guidebook to your area.

On this spot

Age range
Nine to eleven.

Group size
Small groups.

What you need
No special requirements.

What to do
This is a storytelling activity. The idea is to start the story by imagining what might have happened at a certain spot in the school grounds.

First talk to the children about the use of commemorative plaques to mark places where someone famous was born or lived for some time, or where something extraordinary happened. If there are any such plaques near your school, take the children to look at them.

Ask the children to suggest plaques they might like to put up. What sort of people or events would they like to commemorate? Can they think of any funny or silly plaques that could be put up – to commemorate something going terribly wrong, for example?

Now ask the children to imagine that in a certain spot in the school grounds something very unusual has happened. Each group has to decide what it was and where it took place. It might be something sinister: on this spot a ghost may have appeared. Or it might be something ridiculous: on this spot the Prime Minister might have slipped on a banana skin when visiting the school.

When each group has agreed on the location and the story, ask the children to practise telling it in their groups. Finally ask each group to tell the others about their spot and why it is famous.

Follow-up
● If the school has a kiln, the children could make their own plaques.
● They could also find out about any famous people or events in their local history. If your school is named after someone, the children might like to research who he or she was.

A letter to the future

Age range
Nine to eleven.

Group size
Individuals or pairs.

What you need
Notepads, sugar paper, wax crayons, pencils, pens.

What to do
Children are often asked to write a description without being shown how to observe detail first. The point of this activity is to get them to look at their school with new eyes and to write about what they have seen.

Talk to the children about the past and the future. Can they find out what the school was like in the past? Are there any old photographs of the school and its pupils? How have lessons changed? Ask the children to think about what life will be like in the future. Will people still drive around in cars? Will there still be trees and grass and flowers? What will people eat? Where will they live? Will the children go to school? What will they think when they read about us?

Ask the children to imagine that it has become possible to send messages to people in the future and for them to send messages to us. Ask them to imagine that they have a pen-friend in the future. Read out the following letter to the children.

Dear Pen-friend,

I am writing to ask you to tell me all about your life in Britain in the twentieth century. I am doing a project on how people lived in the past. I find it hard to imagine what it is like for you. In history lessons, the computer says that your lives were very hard, that you had no robots to do the work and that you had to go to something called school all day.

Please write back and describe your school. I want to imagine what it was like. Tell me everything about it – what it looked like, what it was built of, the colours, the shapes.

I am looking forward to getting your letter.

With best wishes,
Ziggy

Take the children outside and ask them to choose a place in the grounds from which to describe the school. Tell them to spend some time looking before they begin their description. Ask them to think about adjectives to describe what they see. Is the wall brick, stone, big, stuccoed, crumbling? Is the path uneven, paved, cracked, overgrown? Is the building large, brick, concrete, new, old?

They could begin their letter like this:

Dear Ziggy,
You wanted to know what my school is like.
Well, if you were standing where I am this is what you would see...

Follow-up

Make a display of the letters on a large sheet of sugar paper. The children might like to draw pictures of Ziggy and his school. They could also write Ziggy's reply.

If some of the children have already got pen-friends, they could bring in their letters and read them to the class. You might also be able to arrange new pen-friends for the children by contacting a class teacher in another school, perhaps even abroad.

You might like to read *Limited Damage* published by Learning Through Landscapes, in which children from the future visit a contemporary school. There are a number of other stories about children who find themselves in a different time. A good example is *Tom's Midnight Garden* Philippa Pearce (1983) Oxford University Press or *The Children of Winter* Berlie Doherty (1985) Methuen.

Mathematics

Identifying shapes and angles

Age range
Five upwards.

Group size
The whole class.

What you need
Chalk.

What to do
Young children's grasp of shapes such as triangles, squares and rectangles, can be enhanced by taking them for a walk in the school grounds and asking them to pick out shapes in the buildings and grounds. Windows and doors will be quickly identified as rectangles or squares. Other shapes may be harder to find. What about the site itself, for example? It might be necessary to look at a plan to see what shape it is. Pay attention to the less likely places such as archways over doors or chimneys. It might help to give the children chalk to draw the shapes on the tarmac.

Older children could also look at the angles that buildings make, as well as those made by the lines drawn on the playground. What sort of angles are they? Can they estimate the size of an angle? Ask them to measure the angle, working in pairs. How accurate was their estimate?

What shapes are there in the paving? Or in the brickwork? Do they tesselate? How do they compare with natural shapes and patterns, like flower petals? Are there any old photographs or plans of the school that you can look at with the children? Have any changes been made since?

Follow-up
● The children could make a model of the school grounds using cardboard packaging. It might help to start with some simple work such as drawing plans of everyday objects.
● You might also like to look at related activities in this book, like 'A tesselation mural' on page 29 and 'History on your doorstep' on page 58.

Snakes and ladders

Age range
Five to eleven.

Group size
The whole class, small groups and pairs.

What you need
If your school does not already have number ladders or number snake markings you will have to either chalk your own or get them painted using durable, non-toxic paint. Many county grounds maintenance teams have templates for, and experience of marking out playgrounds. Most county supplies catalogues carry the appropriate paint for do-it-yourself schemes.

Many secondary art and design departments would welcome a real task linked to environmental and personal and social education. You might be able to get their assistance.

What to do
In some cases, children will need initial prompting to use playground markings. Any sort of number work will spring to life when they actually walk it out or stand on the numbers. Children often need simply to be introduced to the markings and they will find more and more uses for them.

A number ladder is a good way of helping younger children learn to recognise the numbers 0–9. They can jump on to the number that has been called out or they can use dice to generate numbers. Once the childen have become familiar with 0–9 sequence, they can use snakes of longer sets such as 0–20 or 0–30.

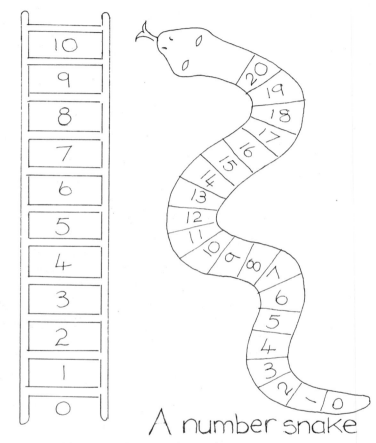

A number ladder

A number snake

Follow-up
The children might like to experiment with different ways of generating the numbers such as using calculators or multiplication tables. They might also like to play hopscotch as described on page 23.

Hopscotch

Age range
Five upwards.

Group size
Two to four.

What you need
To encourage the children to work with numbers, introduce them to a new form of hopscotch. Most children know the rules of this game which are as follows:

The first child throws a pebble, aiming to land it on square 1. If successful, she jumps on to the table, missing square 1 and landing with a foot in each double square, for example, 2 and 3, but hopping on one foot only on to single squares, for example, 4.

At the top of the table, she turns round and comes back again. When she reaches squares 2 and 3, she picks up the pebble and jumps back to the start, missing out square 1. She then throws the pebble again, aiming for square 2 and carrying on until she misses a square with the pebble or lands incorrectly.

When the first player's turn is interrupted, the second player takes over. He jumps through the table avoiding his own square and the square the first player is still trying for.

The winner is the first one to complete all the numbers. The game can be played by any number of players. Obviously, the more players there are, the more squares have to be avoided. It gets very difficult with more than four players at a time.

Very young children will find hopscotch useful for recognising numbers and their order. Older children can use two dice to generate numbers. They can perform whatever operations are necessary with the thrown numbers to achieve the required number. For example, if the number needed were three and the two dice showed six and three, subtraction could produce the result. If the numbers thrown were two and one, they could be added. If the number needed were six and the dice showed three and two, they could be multiplied and so on.

The children could write down a record of their operations.

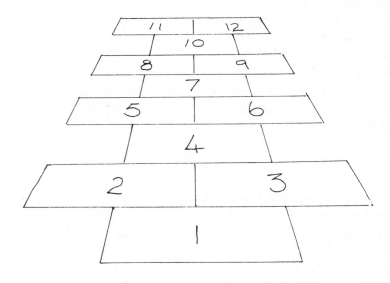

Follow-up
What other hopping or skipping games using numbers could the children design? What other games can be made up for a hopscotch grid?

A hundred square

Age range

Five to eleven.

Group size

The whole class, small groups and pairs.

What you need

A hundred square marked out on the playground (see comment for 'Snakes and ladders' on page 22); you may also like to add compass directions and numbers and letters along the sides for use in grid work, as shown in the illustration below.

What to do

A hundred square is the most versatile number game of all. After playing it for a very short time, children will be able to pick out a variety of number patterns.

Ask the children to subtract or add, count in twos or threes or higher numbers and to stand a member of the class on the number generated. Talk about the patterns they have noticed. Ask them to stand on all the even numbers, all the odd numbers, all the numbers which are multiples of three or seven, or have three or seven in them, and so on.

Grid work is another area that can be made more exciting with active games.

Ask the children to find grid references for a given number or to stand on the numbers at given grid references. This can be expanded to include puzzles such as this one: multiply the number at A3 by the number at B1. Give the grid reference for your answer.

Directional work can be pursued alone or in combination with numbers. Here are some examples.
- Start at number 16. Move 3 squares north, 4 squares south-west and 1 square east. Where do you end up?
- If you were standing on number 76 which direction would you have to follow to reach number 32? How far?

A HUNDRED SQUARE

Follow-up

You can use chalk or paint to add details to the hundred square. Here are some suggestions.

- Mark every multiple of five with a symbol, for example, a triangle or a star.
- Mark every multiple of ten with a different symbol.
- Jumble up the letters of the alphabet and put them in the corners of the boxes.

For real brain-teasers, you can combine all of the above. You can either devise some yourself or the children can make them up for each other, combining all the elements – grid references, compass directions, letter and number puzzles. Here are some examples.

- Give the grid references that spell out your name.
- If you wanted to spell out the word COMPASS, where should you start, what direction should you take and by how many steps? Give all the instructions in sequence.

You and the children could design other marking systems, using concentric circles, spirals, triangles or number lines.

Leaf sizes

Age range
Seven to eleven.

Group size
The whole class.

What you need
1cm squared paper, sugar paper and felt-tipped pens.

What to do
Take the children for a walk in the school grounds. Ask them to collect one or more leaves each. These can be leaves of plants, but tree leaves would be much better. Encourage the children to look for fallen leaves on the ground rather than pluck still-growing ones. If there are no plants or trees growing in your school grounds, try the local park.

It might help to talk beforehand about the way leaves provide the tree or plant with energy by soaking up sun-rays. In preparation for the following activity, explain that the size of the leaf is an important factor in the amount of energy absorbed.

Ask the children to place the leaf on 1cm squared paper and to draw around it. They can measure the area of the leaf by counting the number of squares inside the outline. Part squares should be counted as half, or as nothing if they are very small. This might be a good time to talk about rounding numbers up or down.

When all the children in the class have measured their leaves, explain that what they have measured is a sample. Leaves from the same tree may vary in size and, of course, leaves from different kinds of trees vary enormously.

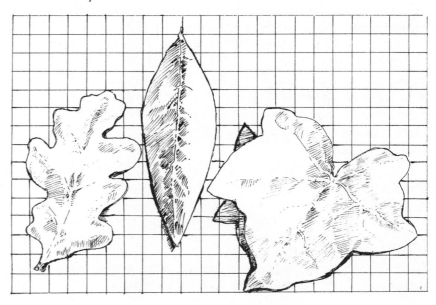

You might like to extend the work to include averages. If the children have measured three leaves each, they could add up their respective areas and divide the total area by three. Or, if they have all measured the leaves from the same tree, why not find the average for the class? Although it is still only a sample, it should give quite a good indication of the average size of leaf of that species of tree.

The results could be displayed in a bar chart on paper or on computer. The children should write the number of leaves along the side axis and the number of squares in groups of 20–25, 25–30, for example, along the bottom axis. This way they can find the mode – the group with the largest number of leaves in it.

Follow-up
The children could prepare a display of the information they have gathered. Why not mount it on a large-scale model of a leaf? This can be made by taking the co-ordinates of a drawing of the leaf shape and reproducing them on a larger grid.

A tree survey

Age range
Seven to eleven.

Group size
Small groups.

What you need
Graph paper, a simple tree guide, tape measure, pencils, a notebook, string, a stick or a ruler.

What to do
This activity will vary according to the time of year. Children will be looking at the shape, size, buds, bark and the type of leaves, depending on the season and the species of tree. If your site has no trees, you can adapt this activity to suit a walk in a local park or street. It may act as an incentive for your school to consider planting trees.

Before you start, make sure that the children are familiar with the basic parts of a tree. If you are conducting your survey in winter, you may also want to explain the idea of evergreen and deciduous trees.

Ask the children to choose an area of the school grounds and to make a map of it on graph paper, marking in major landmarks such as paths and buildings. You might want to talk about the concept of scale and measurement throughout this activity. Some children may be able to work out a scale for their map at this stage.

The children should now mark in all the trees. It helps to be systematic, adding each tree in a set order and numbering it on the map. The map might look like this:

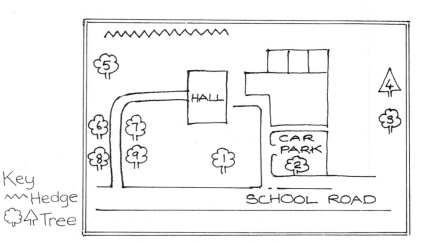

Tree is three times
the height of child
who is 1½ metres
∴ tree is about
4½ metres high

Using a tree guide and your help, the children should be able to describe and identify as many trees as possible. Even if they cannot identify all of them, they can measure their girth and estimate their height. They can enter all their findings on the reproducible pages in the School Grounds Survey on pages 108-113.

To measure a tree's girth, use the string to surround it at chest height. You could also use the outstretched arms of a number of children if you are lucky enough to have large trees on your site or in your area. This activity can lead to work with non-standard measurements and to the idea of circumference.

To estimate the height of a tree, get the children to work in pairs. One child should stand next to the tree, which the other, at some distance, holds up a stick or a ruler vertically at arm's length and moves her thumb up and down it until the top of the stick is in line with her friend's head and the bottom with her feet. The stick should then be marked. Using this part of the stick as a rough guide, the first child should now work out how

many times it goes into the height of the tree by holding it at arm's length and moving it up the height of the tree. To get the approximate height, the child should multiply this number by the height of the friend next to the tree as in the illustration above.

Follow-up

● Further survey work could be conducted on birds, squirrels and insects in the trees. Groups of children could keep seasonal illustrated diaries of their observations. The maps can be coloured and labelled and individual trees drawn in greater detail.

● The children might like to make scale maps showing trees in their gardens or neighbourhoods. These might be presented as a class display.

Bird count

Age range
Seven to eleven.

Group size
The whole class.

What you need
A bird-table (see page 49 for instructions).

What to do
Observing animals gives a real context and purpose to maths operations. Birds in particular invite an enormous number of activities which can be recorded in a variety of ways, giving the children the opportunity to learn about birds while engaging in 'real' maths. However, it is worth pointing out that birds are unlikely to visit a school simply because it has a bird-table. They need the whole site to be friendly to their needs for food and shelter.

Ask the children to record at regular intervals, perhaps every hour, the number of birds visiting the table. If you have already done some work on recognising different species, the children should be able to tell the birds apart.

Ask the children to plot the results on a bar chart like the one below. Can they discover any connections between the times of greatest use and the events in the school day such as break times?

If you have erected more than one bird-table, you can compare the usage of each. What factors might account for one table being used more than another?

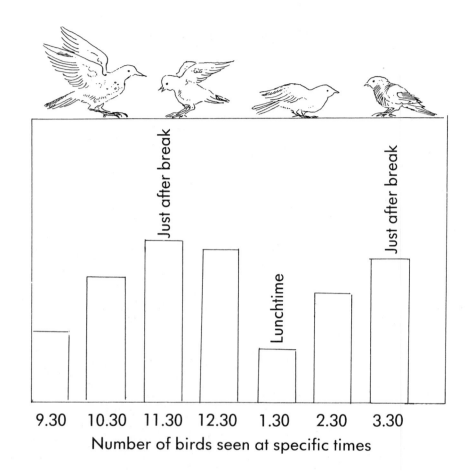

Number of birds seen at specific times

Follow-up
● The Royal Society for the Protection of Birds have produced a set of resources for developing mathematical skills and concepts through studies of wild birds. See Resources, page 127 for further details.
● You may also try a similar exercise with other animals, for example, slugs or worms. The children will have to decide on a specific location to make their count.

A tessellation mural

Age range
Seven to eleven.

Group size
Small groups.

What you need
Two-dimensional shapes, cardboard, scissors, a ruler, non-toxic outdoor paint, paintbrushes, large felt-tipped markers or chalks, masking tape.

What to do
Before you start this activity, you will need to obtain permission from the headteacher. You might also like to speak to the school's landlord.

Explain to the children that they are going to paint a mural to brighten up the playground. Talk to them about tessellation, allowing them to experiment with two-dimensional shapes to find out which ones tessellate. Tell the children which colours are available and ask them to draw their designs.

Agree on what the final overall design will look like. Depending on the size of the wall, you could divide it into as many sections as there are children and mark up each section with one child's design. Alternatively, you could pick one overall design by drawing one name out of a hat. In either case, you will probably need to enlarge the scale of the children's original design.

Ask the children to make their own large cardboard templates of the shapes in their patterns. Ask them to practise tracing round the templates and to paint the resulting patterns.

Mark out a rectangle of wall for each child. You might find it helpful to separate the rectangles with masking tape.

Ask the children to draw round their templates with felt-tipped markers or chalks, depending on the surface, and to paint their patterns in the allocated spaces.

Follow-up
Take the children to look at mosaics and tile patterns in a local museum. You could also extend the activity into areas of art, for example, by making a class mosaic with the children. One way of obtaining mosaic material is to paint blown eggs and then to break them into pieces.

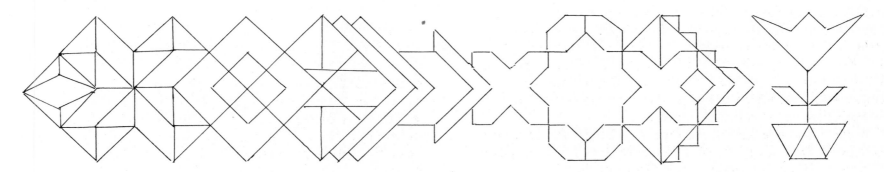

Measuring water usage

Age range
Seven to eleven.

Group size
Small groups.

What you need
Buckets, calculators, a stop-watch.

What to do
This activity shows the children how much water is used at school.

Start by brainstorming everything that the class knows about water and where it comes from. Children will love fascinating detail, like the fact that the water from the Thames has been recycled through people's kidneys several times, or that the water in the Hudson River in New York is so polluted that it is actually inflammable.

Then start focusing the discussion on the use of water in the school buildings and grounds. Are there any drains and manholes? Are the plants watered regularly? Are there any leaking taps in the lavatories?

Ask the children to calculate how much water is needed to wash hands. They can do this by timing how long it takes them to wash their hands and then allowing the tap to run into a bucket for the same period. If the bucket does not fit into the sink it may be necessary to use a piece of tubing. They could then count how many times a day each child washes her hands while at school and how many children attend the school, in order to calculate how much water the children use every day just to wash their hands.

The children might be able to interview the kitchen staff to find out how much water they use daily. They could calculate how much water the school kitchen uses over a year.

Both activities provide opportunities for estimating, addition, multiplication and averaging. The results can be presented in a number of ways on paper or on computer screen.

Follow-up
● Ask the children to find out about the outside uses of water, such as fountains, carwashes and sprinklers. How much water is required for a single carwash? They might also like to estimate water consumption in their own homes.
● Talk to the children about ways of cutting down on water use, for example, by collecting rainwater for the garden or by making sure there are no leaking taps in the building. Look at the problems faced by societies with no access to running water.

A sponsored playground walk

Age range
Seven upwards.

Group size
The whole class.

What you need
Printed sponsor sheets, a stop-watch, pencils and paper.

What to do
A sponsored walk around your grounds or playground has the advantage of being an activity with a very tangible purpose of raising money for a charity. It can also include a great deal of maths.

First, you will need to decide on the purpose for raising the money. Then discuss the route with the children – this can be anything from a simple circuit of the playground to a planned trail with objects that have to be retrieved at specific points. Discuss with the children how much money they would like to raise. Ask them to get as many sponsors as possible and to work out how much they can raise individually. How much will this make altogether?

Ask the children to estimate how long it will take to complete the course. Then get them to time each other over the course using stop-watches and logging the individual times. Later they can present their findings graphically.

Talk about averages. Find out the average time taken to complete the course.

When all the money has been collected, find out how successful the children have been in meeting their target.

What percentage of the target amount have they collected?

Follow-up
Ask your chosen charity to send you some information about its work and how your money will be used or, better still, to send a representative to talk to the children.

Table hopping

Age range
Five to nine.

Group size
Pairs.

What you need
Chalk – it is probably better to chalk the numbers on the playground rather than have them painted, because you may want to use different tables at different times.

What to do
This is a simple number game to reinforce multiplication tables.

Draw a grid on the ground or pavement – six squares by four is a good size for working on two tables at once.

Put in the numbers. Those shown below will work for the two- and three-times tables. You can devise your own numbers for other tables. Similarly, you can make the table more or less complicated.

The object of the game is to get from one side to the other, jumping from square to square in the correct order. The children should agree first which multiplication table they are working on and take it in turns to jump to the next correct number when the teacher or another player calls out the sum. Jumps can be in any direction, including diagonally.

Follow-up
Give the children squared paper and ask them to devise their own table-hopping squares for two other tables or for more than two tables at once. They might also like to try some of the other number games in this chapter (see pages 22, 23 and 24).

Measuring the school

Age range
Nine to eleven.

Group size
Three to four.

What you need
A trundle wheel, clipboards, paper, pencils, squared paper, rulers.

What to do
Many schools do not appear to have been built with any real awareness of children's need for space. This is particularly true of Victorian schools, but also of many modern ones.

Ask the children to measure the playground in metres using the trundle wheel, then to calculate the area of the playground. It might be easier to do this by first drawing a scale plan on 1cm or 2cm squared paper, using a scale of 1cm or 2cm to 1m, and then counting the squares. How much playground room does this give to each child in the school?

Ask the children to imagine they are re-designing their school grounds. How much playing space would they recommend for each child? How big would this make the playground?

For guidelines on the amount of space required by children for different outdoor activities, you might like to refer to *Building Bulletin 28* (1982) HMSO and *Building Bulletin 71* (1990) HMSO.

Follow-up
Talk to the children about the history of your school. Does it go back a long time? How were children expected to behave in those days? What were the lessons like?

Science

Using a sand-pit

Age range
Five to seven.

Group size
The whole class.

What you need
Sand-pit, buckets and spades, shovels, hose-pipe, magnifying glass.

What to do
Children can learn a great deal about the properties of sand through free play and personal experience. Play sessions with a few basic tools give them the opportunity to experiment with sand on their own.

Ask them to look at sand under a magnifying glass. What is it made up of? Explain how sand is created, where it comes from and where it is found. Is it always by the sea?

Ask the children to build a sand city. Why is it so difficult to make shapes that stay put? What does the expression 'building on sand' mean?

Rig up a hose-pipe between a mains cold-water outlet and the sand-pit. Moisten a patch of sand. Allow the children to use wet sand, as well as dry. Is the wet sand better for building? Why?

Turn the water on and show how the flow of water creates tunnels under the 'city' by erosion. Vary the flow of water. Where does the sand go? Is it deposited a long way away from its original position? What does this tell us about where sand comes from?

Follow-up
● Discuss the uses of sand – as a building material (mortar, sandstone), in glass-making, in egg-timers and so forth.
● Make sand pictures by using glue on pieces of card and sprinkling sand on.
● Make a plan of the grounds marking in all the features where sand is present.

Leaf games

Age range
Five to seven.

Group size
Small groups.

What you need
Magnifying glasses.

What to do
There are many activities which use leaves. They can help children learn to observe and identify.

You can begin by pointing out that leaves of different trees vary in colour, size and shape. A good chart will make this clearer.

Take the children out on a walk near some trees. If your school grounds do not have any, you will have to use the local park. Ask the children to collect four or five leaves each and to study them carefully through a magnifying glass. Talk about their colour and shape.

Ask the children to turn round while you spread out the leaves in a different order. Now ask them to turn round and identify their own leaves.

Another game which has particular appeal for young children is Leaf Snap. You need to tear a number of leaves in half and distribute them to the class who then use them like playing cards to play snap.

Follow-up
You can use the leaves to make prints as described on page 69.

A minibeast habitat

Age range
Five upwards.

Group size
Small groups.

What you need
Pieces of old carpet (not foam-backed) or woollen blanket, screwtop glass jars, paintbrushes, magnifying glasses.

What to do
Talk to the children about the different kinds of minibeasts that they might find. Use a good reference book or series of charts to familiarise them with the characteristics of minibeasts. Discuss their habitats.

Ask the children to place their pieces of carpet on grassy ground and ensure that they are left undisturbed for a week. Return and lift the carpet. What creatures are sheltering there?

Ask the children to try to capture some of the minibeasts using paintbrushes and glass jars. Can they identify them? Looking at them through a magnifying glass will help. Older children could fill in a key to identify their catch, recording number of pairs of legs, body segments, presence or absence of pincers and other significant details.

What has happened to the grass under the carpet? Can the children give reasons for this?

Make sure the children release the minibeasts afterwards.

Follow-up

Ask the children to keep a wildlife diary over a period of time. They might like to create other microhabitats for different types of creatures. A pile of composting vegetation, for example, will often attract centipedes, millipedes and beetles, and provide a larder for hedgehogs. These warm, humid areas should be kept open with a few branches so that there is space for slow-worms and grass snakes to retreat. These are rarer visitors and will only appear if the composting heaps are set in the context of the surrounding landscape.

Shadows

Age range
Five upwards.

Group size
Pairs.

What you need
Chalk, pencils, large sheets of paper.

What to do
Talk to the children about shadows. Ask questions such as the following:
- Can you separate yourself from your shadow?
- Does your shadow change shape?
- Can you have a shadow at night?

A simplified version of this activity for younger children is to ask them, on a sunny day, to trace each other's shadows on paper. One child stands against the sun on the edge of a sheet of paper so that his or her shadow falls on paper, while another child draws around the shape. Explain what causes the shadow. Cut out the shadow shapes and display them in the classroom.

Older children can make a series of recordings of each other's shadows. It is easier to draw directly on to the playground instead of using paper. Ask the children to draw round the feet first and to write the child's initials inside the footprints. This marks the place where each child stood and allows them to return to exactly the same spot. They should draw round the shapes of the shadows at 10 am, 12 am and 2 pm. What conclusions can they draw from the differences?

Follow-up
Talk about the way the Earth and other planets travel round the Sun, the Moon's orbit of the Earth, eclipses of the Sun and Moon. You might even be able to incorporate illustrations of the planets in your playground markings.

Investigating spiders

Age range
Five upwards.

Group size
The whole class.

What you need
Squares of card, PVA medium or other transparent adhesive, string, large plastic sweet jars, paintbrushes, cotton wool.

What to do
Take the children on a spider hunt in the school grounds. Ask them to collect a spider and put it in a jar lined with a piece of damp cotton wool at the bottom to keep the air inside the jar moist. They should use a paintbrush to pick up the spider to avoid damaging it.

The children can observe the spider for the whole day but they should release it before they go home. Talk about what the spider looks like: how many legs does it have? Does it have any wings?

The children can also collect webs by putting glue on the surface of the card and putting the card behind the web very gently, so that the web sticks to the card. They should record where and when they found the web. If they have made a map of the school grounds (see page 26) they can mark on it where they found the webs.

Removing the webs may seem destructive but, in fact, spiders' webs are continually being destroyed by larger animals. It does not take a spider very long to spin another.

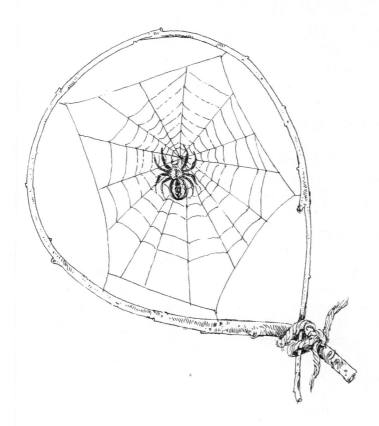

The children could try using the string to recreate the patterns of the spider's web between two posts or two chairs. How easy is it?

Follow-up

There are many songs, stories and poems concerned with spiders. Here are some examples: the traditional nursery rhyme 'Incey Wincey Spider'; *Anancy – Spiderman*, James Berry (1989) Walker Books; *Charlotte's Web*, E. B. White (1969) Puffin Books.

Making a mini-pond

Age range
Five upwards.

Group size
The whole class.

What you need
A half-barrel, an old basin or other similar container, a length of butyl pond liner, four or five old bricks, a saucer, a jam-jar.

What to do
Not all schools are fortunate enough to have their own pond. If yours does not, you can make a mini-pond with a half-barrel and some pond liner.

Talk with the children first about the sorts of creatures that live in ponds. Are all ponds permanent or are some temporary? Which dries out first — a wide, shallow pond or a smaller, deeper one? Experiment with a saucer and a jam-jar to discover the answer.

Discuss the best location for the pond. Arrange the bricks in steps on one side to create a shallow end for frogs and toads. Cover the bricks and the inside of the barrel with the liner. Fill the lined half-barrel with tap-water, then allow it to stand for several days. You could visit a local pond and bring a jar of pond-water back with you to add to your own pond. Observe your pond over a period of time. What animals have come to live in it? Where did they come from? Keep a class diary which describes the changes in the pond.

Follow-up

In summer, examine the surface of your pond for eggs of gnats or mosquitoes. If you find them, put some in a jar. Leave the jar in the grounds and watch them hatch into tiny larvae, or wrigglers. After a few days, the larvae will change into pupae and finally into adult gnats or mosquitoes.

Observing ants

Age range
Five upwards.

Group size
The whole class.

What you need
Some milk-bottle tops, small quantities of sugar, jam, biscuit crumbs and bread, a watch with second-hand.

What to do
Talk to the children about insects in general and about ants. Ask them how many different kinds of ants they have heard of. Are ants pests or do they perform any useful functions? Explain that they are going to carry out an investigation into the eating habits of ants.

Take the children for a walk in the school grounds and ask them to look for an ants' nest. When they have found one, place the milk-bottle tops near by and put small quantities of the different foods in each top. Now ask the children to watch what happens. They should

note how long it takes the ants to discover the food, which food they go to first, which food most ants prefer and whether they attempt to bring any of it back to their nest.

Ask the children to think about how the ants learn of the presence of the food. Can they smell it? Can they see it? Do they communicate with each other about it?

Follow-up

Ask the children to find out as much as they can about ants. Why are there different kinds within one colony? When do flying ants appear and why? What is a queen ant? Which creatures are enemies of ants?

A simple telephone

Age range
Seven to nine.

Group size
Pairs.

What you need
Two empty yoghurt pots, at least 15 metres of string.

What to do
Talk to the children about the problems of communication over long distances. Discuss the different methods that have been used such as smoke signals, carrier pigeons, semaphores, letters, telegraph, Morse code, telephones, telex, fax. What are the advantages and disadvantages of each system? How

are we likely to communicate with each other in the future?

Show the children how to make a playground telephone by piercing a hole in the bottom of each yoghurt pot, threading the string through each pot and tying a knot at either end. When the string is stretched taut, the children will be able to use the system to speak to each other. They can also experiment with changes to the system. Does it make any difference if the string is longer or shorter? If the string is broken or a knot tied in it, does it still work? Explain to the children that sound travels in waves along the string.

Follow-up

● If you have access to an oscilloscope, show the children a picture of the wave forms made by different sounds.
● Experiment with other systems of communication. Can the children devise their own system for passing a simple message from one group to another over a distance?

Kites

Age range

Seven to eleven.

Group size

Pairs.

What you need

Gardening cane or thin dowelling, thread, resin glue, brown wrapping paper, string, paste.

What to do

Children enjoy experiments with hot-air balloons, parachutes, kites, gliders and model aeroplanes. Rather than following complicated instructions to produce an elaborate model, it is better to help the children make a simple version and then go on to modify the basic design.

To make a basic kite, prepare a kite framework out of split cane or thin dowelling, lashing the joints together with cotton thread. Cover thread-bound joints with thin resin glue and allow to dry.

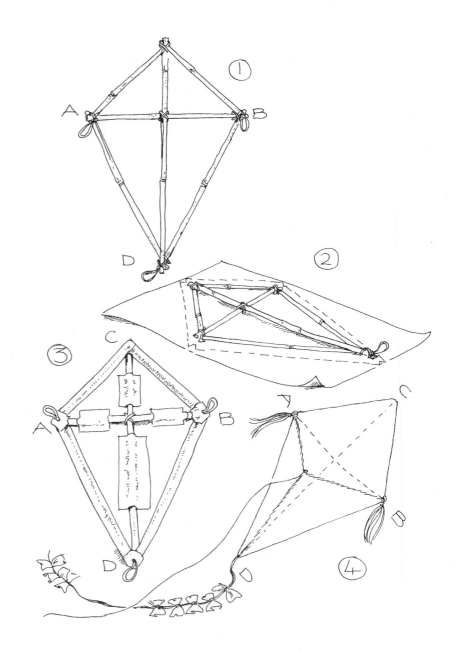

Make strong loops of thin string at points A, B and D (see illustration). Lay the kite down on brown wrapping paper. Cut round the kite shape allowing 3cm overlap. Paste overlap over the edge of the frame on to the paper backing of the kite face. Reinforce with strips of pasted paper over the cross-piece. Reinforce the area round the loops with squares of strong pasted paper by pushing loops through the holes at the centre of reinforcement squares. Attach the bridle at points A, B and D.

Modifications can be made in the type of materials used to make the kites, in their bridle attachments and by the addition of wing-tip tassels and tails of different design.

Follow-up

● Talk about early attempts to build a flying machine, many of which resembled kites. You could take the children to a museum of aviation if there is one in your area.
● You might also make model aeroplanes and gliders and try some simple experiments with parachutes.

A balloon message

Age range
Seven to eleven.

Group size
The whole class.

What you need
A helium-filled balloon, a camera, an envelope, paper, a stamped postcard, a hole puncher, string.

What to do
Take a group photograph of all the children in the class. When it has been developed, show it to them.

Helium balloons can often be bought in the local high street. Bring one into the class and talk about it. Why does it float? Ask the children how far they think it would travel if released on a windy day. Talk about airships, like the *Hindenburg*, and their advantages and disadvantages as a form of transport.

Tell the children they are going to attach a message to the balloon and send it off. Ask them to agree on the contents of the message, which one of the children should write down and put it an envelope, together with the class photograph and a stamped postcard with the school's address and the words 'Time and date found'. Ask all the children in the class to sign the message. Punch a hole in the corner of the envelope and tie it to the balloon with string.

Explain that someone may find the balloon and the attached message and return the children's postcard by post. To avoid disappointment, you should add that it is equally likely that the balloon will drift up into a treetop

or that the finder will forget to post the enclosed card.
Take the children into the school grounds and launch the balloon, recording the time and date of the launch.

Follow-up

If the balloon is returned, mark its journey on a large map, with the length of time taken and the average speed. You might like to repeat the experiment and compare journeys.

Looking closely at soil

Age range
Seven to eleven.

Group size
The whole class.

What you need
A bucket of soil, an old sheet, plastic containers, jam-jars with lids, sticky tape, gloves or thick plastic bags, a spoon, reference books.

What to do
This activity is designed to make the children aware that soil is a complex substance and an important environment on which all life depends.

Start by discussing with the children the importance of soil for human, animal and plant life. Ask the children to imagine what the world would be like if there were no soil.

Go outside and find the nearest bit of soft ground. Look at what is growing there. Look at the different-sized particles in the soil. Feel any stones. Ask the children to bring in the five smallest stones they can find. Mount the stones on sticky tape. Explain what stones are and what they have to do with soil.

Bring in a bucket of soil and tip it out on to a piece of old sheet or plastic. Look for any living creatures. Put them into separate containers and, using reference books, identify them. Get all the children to feel a pinch of soil between their fingers. Ask them to describe it. What does it smell of? Does it stain the hands? Sort out any bits of organic matter. Get them to draw and label their findings.

Put some soil into a jar with a lid. Shake the jar vigorously and see what happens after 30 seconds, 1 minute, 5 minutes, 1 hour, 24 hours, 48 hours (after 48 hours soil will separate out into distinct layers).

To see if there is air in soil, fill a bucket half full with soil. Pour water in until the earth is covered. Show the children small bubbles of escaping air. Have a spoon ready to rescue any small creatures. Stirring the soil with the spoon should produce more air bubbles.

Follow-up

The children can try similar activities with different samples of soil from their gardens or local parks. They should note the results and record them in a class chart.

Investigating litter

Age range
Seven upwards.

Group size
Pairs.

What you need
Clipboards, pencils and paper, chalk, gloves or thick plastic bags.

What to do
Begin by discussing the problems of waste disposal. Where does litter come from? What happens to it when we throw it away?

Ask the children to carry out a litter survey of the school grounds. They should investigate:
● where the most litter accumulates;
● what sort of litter it is — sweet wrappings, crisp packets, newspapers, drink cans and so on;
● what it is made from;
● whether it could be recycled.

The children should wear gloves or thick plastic bags on their hands when picking up litter.

They should also look at the number and location of bins in the school buildings and grounds. Are there enough bins in the areas with the most litter?

In addition, they could carry out a survey among the other children at break time, asking them whether they used the bins, whether they thought the bins were well situated and where else they would like to see them.

Ask them to find a particularly littered area in the school grounds, identify the items in it, write them down,

note the time, then draw a chalk circle around the area. After three hours they should return and see where the litter is now. How widely has it been dispersed? What has moved it?

Finally the children could display the results of their investigations on large display boards in a central area to help make other children aware of the problem of litter. They could also design their own series of anti-litter posters and put them up around the school. They could also be encouraged to develop their own anti-litter slogans.

Follow-up

Invite a speaker in from the Keep Britain Tidy Research group. Also, a visit to your local waste disposal plant might provide graphic evidence of the scale of the problem!

Making flower dyes

Age range
Nine to eleven.

Group size
Pairs.

What you need
A Bunsen burner, a tripod, gauze, a heat-resistant mat, white wool, two beakers, muslin squares, string.

What to do
Some people believe that children should not under any circumstances be encouraged to pick flowers. Explain why they may think so and tell the children that they will be picking only a few cultivated flowers from the school flower-beds. If your school has no flowering plants in the grounds, you will have to buy some different-coloured flowers from a florist's or ask the children to bring them from their gardens at home.

Keep the different colours separate. Cut up the petals into small pieces and wrap them in squares of muslin. Tie the muslin with string and place each bag in a separate beaker filled with cold water. Heat the beakers over a Bunsen burner. Place a length of white wool in each beaker. Allow the water to simmer for half an hour, then turn it off. When the water has cooled down, take out the wool, squeeze it out and allow it to dry.

Some flowers make good dyes on their own, others work better if used with a mordant such as alum.

Follow-up
• Make a dye chart to show which petals make the best dyes. Other parts of plants can also be used, for example, onion skins give a strong golden colour.
• Try tie-dyeing a piece of cotton cloth. Tie knots in it before immersing it in the dye solution. When the knots are untied, the dye will show as irregular concentric patterns.
• You may want to give the children more information on the history and technology of dyeing.

Technology

Building a bird-table

Age range
Five to eleven.

Group size
Pairs.

What you need
Offcuts of plywood about 30cm², beading, screw-eyes, paper, pencils, rulers, string, wood glue.

What to do
There is a tendency to believe that birds and other wildlife will colonise a school site with the support of bird-tables, bat-boxes and such like. In fact, the really exciting developments begin when a range of complementary habitats has been developed: undergrowth, wild-flower meadows, trees and fruit-bearing bushes. However, building and setting up bird-tables can begin this process and will certainly liven up a glum landscape.

Talk to the children about the birds in the school grounds. Can any be seen from the classroom window? Which birds can be identified with the aid of reference books or charts?

Ask the children to think of ways of enticing the birds for more accurate observation. Leaving out food will almost certainly be suggested. Discuss the problems presented by leaving food on the ground for birds. Suggest building a bird-table. Where should it be located? What sort of places should be avoided?

A simple hanging bird-table could be built as follows.

Fix screw-eyes into the four corners of a piece of plywood. Cut beading to fit round all four sides. Glue it in place. Thread string through the screw-eyes. Hang the table on a branch or other suitable point.

The children could try putting out different types of food and record how long it remained, whether or not it suffered damage from the weather, what birds were attracted to the table. Was there any evidence of undesirable animals like cats or squirrels using the table?

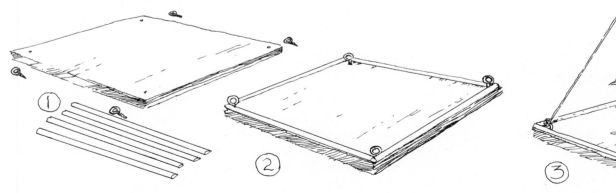

Ask the children to improve on the bird-table design. What factors do they need to take into consideration? Do they need to move a cover for the food? Is the beading high enough to prevent the food from blowing away?

They should do a series of preliminary drawings and then talk about their designs. Are they practical? What materials do they require? How will they be fixed in position? The children could experiment with models using cardboard or packaging.

Follow-up
The Royal Society for the Protection of Birds have produced a range of material for studying birds in the school grounds.

Bottle racing

Age range
Nine to eleven.

Group size
Pairs.

What you need
Plastic lemonade bottles (the ones with rounded bottoms are best), elastic bands, firm wire, nails, beads.

What to do
Talk to the children about transport. Ask questions such as the following:
• How long have we had motor cars?
• How fast were the first motor cars able to go?
• What instrument measures speed in a motor car?

Show the children how to make lemonade-bottle buggies using the following instructions.

Make a small hole in the bottom of the bottle and another one in the bottle top. Knot elastic bands together and thread them through. Anchor them to the bottom of the bottle with a nail.

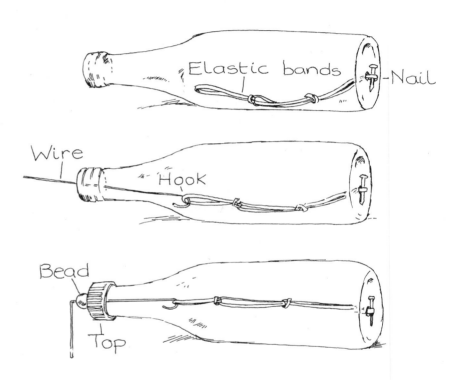

Make a hook in the wire, feed it through the bottle top and the neck of the bottle and hook the other end of the elastic-band chain. Thread the wire through the bottle top and screw the top into place. Thread a bead on to the wire. Bend the wire through 90°.

Wind the buggy up using the wire as a handle. Make sure that the nail stays still. Set the buggy down on the ground, preferably on tarmac, and watch it move forwards.

Ask the children to improve on the design. Can they get the bottle to go straight? What difference does it make if they increase the number of turns given to the elastic? Does the length of the wire make any difference? Does the size of the bottle make any difference? Is it possible to link two buggies together?

Follow-up
When the children have managed to get the buggies to go straight, they can calculate their speed by recording the amount of time it takes them to travel a measured distance.

Making a playground chess set

Age range
Nine to eleven.

Group size
Pairs.

What you need
A chessboard painted on the playground – this could be done by your county grounds maintenance staff or the art and design department of the local secondary school; 32 plastic bottles (sizes to correspond to chess pieces, for example, large lemonade bottles for king and queen); sand or gravel; sandpaper, paint, colour paper, papier mâché, PVA adhesive.

What to do
Before you start this activity, make sure all the children in the classroom are familiar with the rules of playing chess. If there are children who do not know how to play, pair them off with a partner who knows the game well.

Show the children different types of chess sets, some simple, some elaborate. You could also show them photographs of ancient chess sets kept in museums.

To make their own set, the children should take the tops or nozzles off the bottles and fill them half full with sand or gravel. They should next rough up the surface of the bottle to make the papier mâché stick. They can then apply papier mâché, moulding it to form the chosen chess piece.

When the papier mâché has dried, the children can decorate their pieces with paint and coloured paper. It is not necessary to choose black and white – other pairs of contrasting colours will do just as well. A coating of thinned-down PVA adhesive will give the pieces a varnished look and will help protect them from moisture.

When the set is ready and dry, the children can take it to the playground and play chess on their outdoor chessboard.

You will need to remind them to store their chess set indoors once they have finished playing.

Follow-up

The children could organise a chess tournament using their set. They could also design and make a trophy for the winner.

Miniature land yachts

Age range
Nine to eleven.

Group size
Pairs.

What you need
Polystyrene tiles or solid polystyrene packaging, plastic knitting needles, plasticine, adhesive tape, cotton reels, card.

What to do
Cut out the shapes of the yachts from the polystyrene tiles as shown below. The width of the base needs to be about three-quarters of its length. 20cm by 15cm is a good size.

To add wheels, thread a cotton reel on to a knitting needle and tape the needle across the base of the yacht shape. Put another reel on the end of the needle and secure it in place with plasticine. Make another such 'axle' and attach it to the base of the yacht with adhesive. Push a third needle upright into the body of the yacht to act as a mast. Secure the mast with plasticine. Make two holes in a sheet of card and thread it over the mast. Fasten the mast to the base with tape.

You can now hold land yacht races in the playground. A windy day would work best, but the children could create a breeze by blowing or waving a stiff piece of card.

They could also experiment with different shapes and sizes of sails and with placing loads on their yachts.

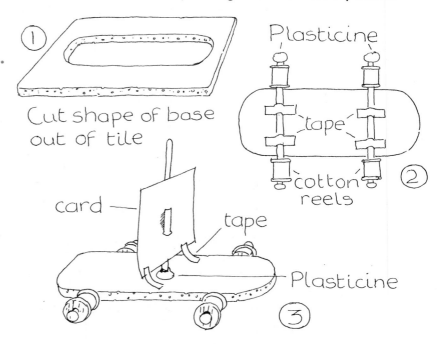

① Cut shape of base out of tile

② Plasticine — tape — cotton reels

③ card — tape — Plasticine

Follow-up

Ask the children to think of other ways of harnessing the wind as a source of power. What are the advantages and disadvantages of wind power?

School signs

Age range
Seven to eleven.

Group size
Small groups.

What you need
Board offcuts and scraps of wood in a variety of shapes and sizes, wooden stakes, non-toxic weatherproof gloss paint and polyurethane varnish, paintbrushes, felt-tipped pens.

What to do
Before you start this activity, you will need permission from your headteachers or the appropriate authority.

First impressions are important for parents and other visitors entering school grounds. Some schools have a friendly and interesting way of 'setting the tone' of their establishment by putting up signs near entrances, paths and driveways.

Discuss the importance of signs with the children. Which ones do they see most commonly? Which ones would they like to see in the school? Which ones would the visitors like to see? Many schools have the word 'Welcome' painted up in a variety of languages. What other signs would make the visitors feel welcome? Are

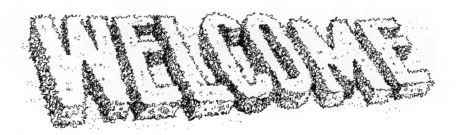

there any aspects of the school the children would like to emphasise?

Ask the children about things that annoy them at school such as dogs fouling the grass or litter dropped. Would a sign help prevent any of them?

The children can design their signs on pieces of board before they transfer them on to wood, by first drawing the outlines with felt-tipped pens and then locking them in with paint.

Younger children will need help with this activity. You could draw the outlines of the letters and let them fill them in with felt-tipped pens. Afterwards, these could be varnished with polyurethane varnish to weatherproof them. The children will need close supervision if they are allowed to varnish the signs themselves.

Together with the children, decide which signs will be appropriate for the school grounds and which could be put up inside the building. For the latter, you may need to get the caretaker's help with drilling holes and fixing the signs up using rawl-plugs and screws. Alternatively, you could fix screw-eyes into the sign, thread twine between and hang it on a nail.

Follow-up
You might like to combine this activity with making a school guidebook, described on page 15.

History

The past is all around you

Age range
Five to seven.

Group size
The whole class.

What you need
Old photographs of the school and its site, old maps of the area, any other evidence of the past use of the site, paper, pencils.

What to do
Introduce the idea of the past with a concrete object such as a photograph of a site or a building with which the children are familiar. Ask them when they think the photograph was taken and what has changed since.

Ask the children to guess the age of the school building. Discuss ways of dating buildings by observing their architectural style and building materials used. Ask them which is older – the school building or its site. It may help to give a local example such as a council estate or a shopping centre built on a site which had to be first demolished or cleared.

Take the children round the school grounds to look for the oldest thing they can find, including trees, hedges and walls. Encourage them to ask questions, even though you may be asked about the age of water, stones or trees which you yourself can only guess. With younger children, you may prefer to ask them to choose one thing which they agree is quite old and to draw it.

Back in the classroom, expand the idea of measuring the age of different objects, both natural and man-made, for example, dating trees by the number of rings in the cross-section of the trunk, or signposts by styles of lettering and types of material used.

Ask the children how old they and their parents were when certain features of the school grounds first appeared. Draw a number of simple time-lines showing the ages of the children and their families and the important dates in the history of the school site.

The purpose of this activity is to stimulate interest in the history of the school site. Before you start, you may want to carry out some basic research of your own. Old school magazines and photographs, newspaper cuttings or, ideally, a school log book, are all rich sources of information. How you develop this session will largely depend on the age of your class and the particular features of your site.

Follow-up

Once the children have grasped the basic concept of time and place, you can introduce them to the idea of time travel. Ask them to imagine they are in a particular year in the past (choose a year with strong local or national historical significance). The way in which the children tackle this concept will give you an idea of how well they have grasped the concept of history.

Burying a time capsule

Age range

Seven to eleven.

Group size

The whole class.

What you need

A large airtight container (plastic or glass), assorted photographs and magazine cuttings, a plastic bag, masking tape, paper, crayons.

What to do

Talk to the children about the concept of a time capsule. Explain that they are going to bury theirs in the school

grounds for someone to dig up in a hundred years' time. Explain that it should contain items that will show the people who open it how we lived. It will help to talk about ways in which our daily life has changed over the past hundred years. What did children wear a hundred years ago? What were their hairstyles like? What did they eat?

Ask the children how we can let the people who will open the time capsule know what we look like, where we live and go to school and what we eat. Ask them to make a selection of photographs and magazine cuttings. The children might also like to write down some school menus or describe a Sunday lunch at home, and to make drawings of themselves or their friends.

When all the items have been chosen, put them in the plastic bag and seal with masking tape. The children can now place the bag in an airtight container and choose a site for the burial. Ensure that they bury the capsule several feet below the surface to avoid it being discovered earlier than planned.

Ensure that the event is a special occasion – you might invite your local newspaper to send a reporter who will provide a written record of the burial. You might also like to mount a plaque on the school wall to mark the site, having first obtained permission from the headteacher.

Follow-up
Contact your local history society or visit a local museum to find out about any artefacts found in your area. What do they tell us about their owners?

A time-line

Age range
Nine to eleven.

Group size
The whole class.

What you need
A trundle wheel, a metre rule, chalk.

What to do
Children often have considerable difficulty with the concept of historical time. Pacing it out on a time-line is a good way of making this clearer.

You might like to get a line properly painted on the playground or you could use one that has been put there for games. Explain the principle of the time-line to the children and ask them to measure the line. Then decide what scale you will use. For example, a period of 3,000 years can be shown on a line 15 metres long, using a scale of 1 metre: 200 years. This scale will be enough to

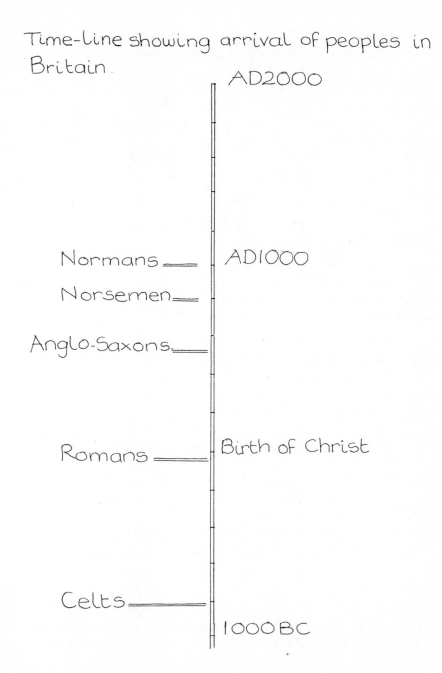

Time-line showing arrival of peoples in Britain.

AD2000

Normans — AD1000

Norsemen —

Anglo-Saxons —

Romans — Birth of Christ

Celts —

1000 BC

show the period from the coming of the Celts to Britain to the present day.

A time-line allows the children to see the process of recording time BC and AD. Talk about the meaning of these abbreviations and why the birth of Christ is taken as the central reference point in the Western world. You might also want to explain the Jewish and Muslim reference points.

Once you have marked in the reference dates, ask the children to mark with chalk the dates you wish to highlight. If they are working on a theme like transport, drawing a time-line will show graphically the acceleration of development in the twentieth century.

Follow-up
The children could draw up time-lines on a theme of their choice. They might also like to suggest alternative central reference points.

History on the doorstep

Age range
Nine to eleven.

Group size
Small groups.

What you need
No special requirements.

What to do
Take the children on an investigation of the school building and grounds. See what evidence they can find of the history of the school.

Many Victorian schools have separate boys' and girls' entrances. What does this tell us about attitudes towards boys and girls in the nineteenth century?

You might like to look for subsequent additions to the school building. Few Victorian schools, for example, have been left as they were originally built. Flat-roofed extensions are common. There is great opportunity here to talk about the sensitivity (or lack of it) of these additions.

Some older schools display insignia of a now defunct education board. In city schools, borders of the old county which established the school may have changed. Schools may also be named after a feature of the environment no longer in existence, or after a notable individual or organisation.

It is also worth looking for features such as boot scrapers (what do they tell us about the state of the roads?), coal sheds, chimneys or bell towers.

See if you can find water and sewerage inspection

holes in the school grounds. Some have elegant cast-iron covers from which children can make wax rubbings and many covers show dates when they were installed.

When the children have assembled their evidence, they can begin to write a history of their school.

Follow-up
The children could find out more about the style of teaching when the school was first founded, as well as the home life of the children who studied there.

Geography

Watching the river flow

Age range
Five to seven.

Group size
The whole class.

What you need
Sand, a hosepipe.

What to do
Talk about how rivers start. Discuss the ways in which they carve out beds for themselves and then gradually erode their banks as they become larger.

Choose a sloping part of the playground. Spread out the sand in a long channel. Ask the children to carve a river bed out of the sand, using their fingers. Encourage them to give it plenty of twists and turns.

Connect the hosepipe to a cold-water supply and place the other end at the head of the river bed. Turn the water on very gently. Ask the children to observe the way the water erodes the banks.

Follow-up
Take the children to see your local river to observe river-bed erosion and how it has been dealt with.

Camels and riders

Age range
Five to seven.

Group size
Pairs.

What you need
No special requirements.

What to do
Talk to the children about the points of compass. Find out which way your school points. Ask them to find out in which direction the sun rises and in which direction it sets.

Talk to them about wind. Ask questions such as the following:
• Does the wind always blow from the same direction?
• Do winds which blow from different directions differ in strength, coldness and dryness?

If there is a weather-vane on your school or a nearby building, keep a regular record of wind direction. You could even ask the children to design and build their own weather-vane and choose a location for it.

Talk about tornadoes and hurricanes. What is the scale we use to describe their strength? Where do they occur and what damage can they do? What steps can be taken to prevent sand drifting and erosion in desert countries?

Investigating puddles

Age range
Seven to eleven.

Group size
Pairs.

What you need
String, beakers of water.

What to do
Talk to the children about the water cycle, how rain is formed and what happens to it when it reaches the ground.

On a sunny day, take the children out into the playground. Explain to them that they are going to carry out a controlled investigation of a puddle. Give each pair a beaker of water and tell them to create their own puddles. When they have poured the water out on the ground, ask them to measure the perimeter of the puddle using string. They should record the measurement and the time it was taken.

Ask them to repeat the measurement at regular intervals. What happens to the puddle? Do some puddles shrink more rapidly than others? What reasons could there be for this?

Discuss the effects of wind on different areas. What is a strong wind at sea called? What does it do to the sea? What would be the effect of wind in the desert?

Take the children out in to the playground to play Camels and Riders. This is a game which is designed to reinforce the concept of wind direction. Make sure everyone is certain which way is north, which south, east and west. Divide the class into pairs. Ask the children to imagine that they are in the desert. One is the rider and one is the camel. Tell them to gallop about until the teacher calls out the direction from which the wind is blowing. Then the children should stop immediately. The camel kneels down and the rider shelters from the wind behind the camel. After a while the camel and the rider swap round.

Making a weather station

Age range
Seven to eleven.

Group size
Pairs.

What you need
For the wind sock: a plastic bin liner, string, a curtain ring, a compass; for the Stevenson's screen: a wooden box, four wooden posts, louvre panelling, two hinges, screws, a screwdriver, a hammer, nails, a saw, a tape-measure, a drill; for the anemometer: four yoghurt pots, two lengths of flat beading, a large nail, a candle, a stapler, a drill, a hammer, strong PVA adhesive or a glue gun; for the rain gauge: a plastic lemonade bottle, scissors; for recording data: a maximum-minimum thermometer, clipboards, seaweed, paper and pencils.

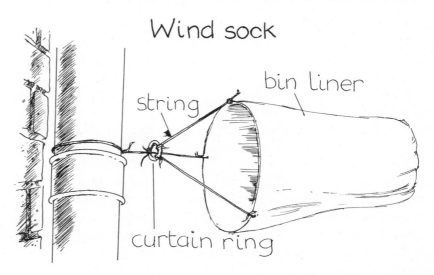

Wind sock

Follow-up
Ask the children to make the puddles larger by stamping in them. Explain about water finding its own level.

Stevenson's screen

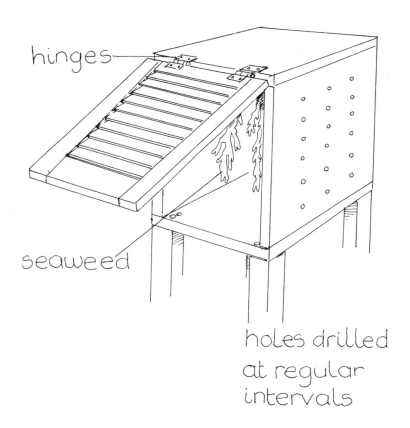

hinges

seaweed

holes drilled
at regular
intervals

posts secured with nails
from inside

Anemometer

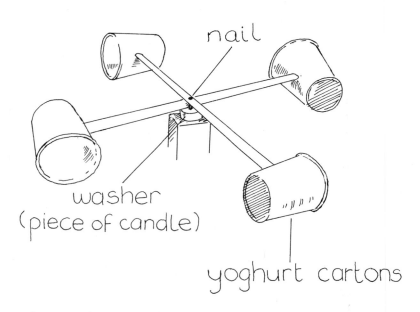

nail

washer
(piece of candle)

yoghurt cartons

What to do

This activity will require close supervision, especially with the younger children, as it involves cutting and drilling wood and using a hammer.

Setting up your own weather station is very easy. You can make a wind sock by attaching three lengths of string to a plastic bin liner, securing them to a curtain ring and adding another length of string from the ring to a post (see illustration).

To make the Stevenson's screen, attach the posts to the box with the open face forwards by nailing through from inside the box. Attach long strips of seaweed to the inside of the top panel so that they hang down. Measure the open face of the box and cut the louvre panelling to

Rain gauge

Lemonade bottle

shown in the illustration. The gauge should be partially buried in the ground, to prevent it from being blown away, but its funnel needs to be about 30cm above ground level to stop rain splashing in from the ground.

Follow-up

● The children could record two or more features of the weather, for example, wind direction and rainfall, over a period of time. These could be presented on a weather chart. Encourage the children to devise their own symbols for the chart.
● You might like to record this activity by filming the children with a video camera when they present their weather reports.

fit. Attach it to the side of the top panel with the hinges. Drill holes in the sides at regular intervals to allow air and moisture through.

The anemometer can be made by gluing two pieces of beading into a cross. If your school has invested in a glue gun, older children could do it themselves under supervision. Allow it to dry, then glue or staple a yoghurt pot on the end of each arm. Cut a section of candle about two centimetres long. Drill a hole slightly larger in diameter than the nail through the centre of the cross. Finally secure the whole thing to a post with a nail, placing the washer between the cross and the post.

To make a rain gauge, cut off the top third of a lemonade bottle and invert it into the bottom third as

Art

The Ugly Bug Ball

Age range
Five to seven.

Group size
The whole class.

What you need
Colouring materials such as paint, wax crayons and oil pastels; card and paper.

What to do
This activity is designed to use minibeasts as a source of inspiration for art activities.

Take the children for a walk in the school grounds and ask them to draw a detailed picture of one of the minibeasts they have spotted. Return to the classroom and give each child a photocopy of the invitation to the ball (see illustration below). Alternatively, the children could design their own invitations.

Ask the children to study their drawings of minibeasts and to design costumes for the Ugly Bug Ball using card and colouring materials of their choice.

This activity could be combined with the following activities in the Science chapter: 'A minibeast habitat', page 36; 'Investigating spiders', page 38; and 'Making a minipond', page 39.

Follow-up
In dance and music sessions, create a choreographed piece for the bugs, to allow the children to explore how insects move. You could use claves and other instruments to experiment with noises made by different insects.

Tarmac blackboards

Age range
Five to seven.

Group size
Small groups.

What you need
Coloured chalk, a large brush, water.

What to do
In many schools children are positively discouraged from chalking on the tarmac, but the reasoning behind this is often left uninvestigated. In fact, children can make considerable advances drawing and writing in this way. Their sense of ownership of the school grounds is also significantly enhanced. Finally, it is worth

pointing out that chalk is easily removed from tarmac by brushing off, especially if a bit of water is used.

Allocate a flat area of the tarmac to the children. You might want to provide them with ideas for drawing such as geometrical shapes or letters of the alphabet, or let them rely on their own inspiration.

Follow-up
Talk to the children about pavement artists. If possible, invite one who works with chalk or pastels to the school grounds.

Making a natural paint chart

Age range
Five to eleven.

Group size
Individuals or pairs.

What you need
Coloured paint charts, pieces of card, double-sided adhesive tape or an adhesive stick.

What to do
The purpose of this activity is to open children's eyes to the range of colours around them. It is particularly effective in late summer and autumn, but will work at any time of the year. It is easily adapted to most urban environments.

Start by introducing the children to different types of paint charts such as those showing all the colours and those which group together families of colours. Ask the children what various colours mean to them, which colours they prefer and why. Tell them they are going on a kind of collecting walk to make their own paint charts from small parts of plants and leaves found in the grounds. Put two or three strips of double-sided adhesive tape on each child's card. Alternatively, use an adhesive stick. You may want to ask the children not to pick growing plants or leaves. Schools have different views on this matter – some allow children to pick only what they have helped to plant. The important thing is to ask the children to be sensitive about their task and to pick only what they need. It is worth reminding the children that even different types of grass and weeds can make very effective 'green' charts. It sometimes helps to specify the number of items to be collected and allow for times when everyone comes together to check on progress.

When the children have made their charts, ask them to talk to the whole class or small groups about their choices.

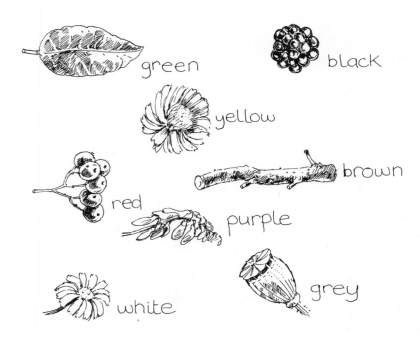

Follow-up

- Let the children display their charts and continue to explore the idea of putting different colours together in other ways, using paint, fabric or a collage of textures.
- You might also like to combine this activity with 'Making flower dyes' on page 47.

Bark rubbings and leaf prints

Age range
Five to eleven.

Group size
Pairs.

What you need
A4-sized paper, wax crayons, paint, latex adhesive.

What to do
If there are trees growing in your school grounds, take the children to visit them. If not, take them to your local park. Show the children how to make bark rubbings by placing paper against the bark and rubbing it with a wax crayon.

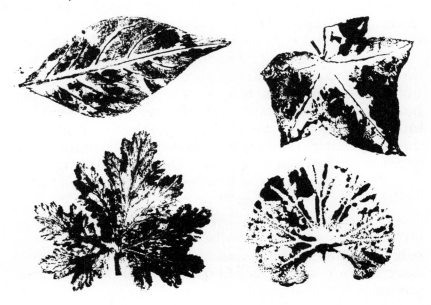

Ask the children to collect a number of different leaves and to bring them back to school. Leaf prints can be made in a number of different ways. Crude imprints can be obtained by painting the leaves and printing directly on to paper. More delicate images can be obtained by gluing the leaves on to paper with a small amount of latex adhesive, then placing another sheet on top and pressing it between the pages of the telephone directory. After a fortnight the leaves will have left their imprints on the paper.

Follow-up

The children could make their own leaf stencils by outlining the leaves on cardboard and cutting out the resulting shapes. These could be used for more complex designs, for example, printing on to T-shirts using a silk screen or fabric crayons.

Plaster casts of natural objects

Age range
Seven to eleven.

Group size
Pairs.

What you need
A selection of small natural objects, plaster of Paris, a shoebox, clay, scissors, paints, a roller.

What to do
Take the children for a walk in the school grounds or in the local park. Ask them to collect items such as acorns, small twigs, leaves, feathers, conkers and pebbles. When you return to the classroom, give each child a piece of clay to roll out flat, like pastry. Ask the children to press the objects into the flattened clay and then remove them.

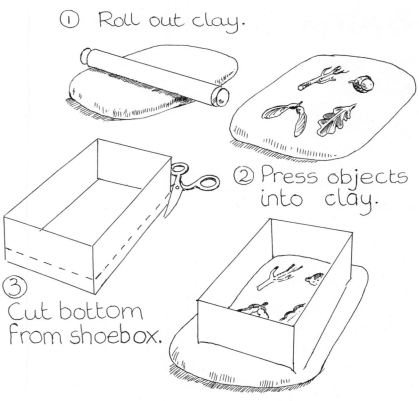

① Roll out clay.

② Press objects into clay.

③ Cut bottom from shoebox.

④ Place box over clay to form mould.

Cut the bottom out of the shoebox and put the sides over the clay to make a mould. Mix the plaster and pour it into the mould.

When the plaster is dry, remove the box and the clay. Paint and display your plaster casts.

Follow-up

Talk about how fossils are created and what we can learn from them. Bring in some fossils or take the children to a museum which has a fossil display.

Above and below

Age range
Nine to eleven.

Group size
The whole class.

What you need
Sketching boards, paper, wax crayons, pencils.

What to do
Asked to draw their surroundings, many children do not know what to draw. This activity is designed to make them aware of their immediate environment.

Take the children into the school grounds. Ask them to observe all the things above their eye level: the sky, clouds and their patterns, birds, aeroplanes and vapour trails; the roofs of buildings and the shapes of aerials and chimneys against the skyline; treetops. If it is a warm, dry day and if there is some grassy surface, ask the children to lie on their backs and look up at the sky.

Then ask them to observe everything they can see below eye level: the surfaces on the ground such as brick, tarmac, earth, grass and puddles; footprints; stones; insects; playground markings. Ask the children to crouch down and examine things very closely. Do they look different?

Now ask the children to pick their own spots and draw what they see from their chosen perspective.

Follow-up
Take photographs of different parts of the school grounds. Concentrate on getting unusual angles. When you have had them developed, make photocopies and give one each to the children, working in pairs. Ask them to locate the areas in the photographs.

Serial vision

Age range
Nine to eleven.

Group size
The whole class or pairs.

What you need
Camera, film, paper, pencils.

What to do
Learning to see is often neglected. More emphasis is placed on making, doing and expressing. This activity is about the way we see the space we pass through.

Decide upon a fixed point in your school grounds. A high point like a weather-vane is a good choice.

Take the children through a number of different routes to the chosen reference point, stopping at intervals and pointing it out to them. Each approach will show a different view of the object – it might be partially hidden by the corner of a building, for example. Depending on the approach taken, the objects around the chosen one will stand in a different relationship to it and to each other: for example, now you might be able to see one of the steps leading up to the main entrance, now two and now three.

Ask the children to choose three different views of the chosen object and to sketch them. Make it clear that the objects in the picture will be the same each time, or almost the same, but the relationships between them will have changed.

You may wish to use a similar technique with a camera. Give the camera to a pair of children and ask

Exploring sound

Age range
Five to seven.

Group size
The whole class or individuals.

What you need
A selection of tuned and untuned instruments, a beater, A4-sized paper, pencils.

What to do
Take the children for a walk in the school grounds. Ask them to stand very quietly with their eyes closed for a few minutes. How many different sounds can they hear? Let them draw a picture of the object that is making the sound. Some sources of sounds, such as the wind, will not be visible. Encourage the children to think of ways of representing them in their drawings. Throughout this activity ensure that the children use musical vocabulary, introducing new terms when necessary.

Back in the classroom, seat the children in a circle. Place a selection of musical instruments in the centre of the circle. Choose instruments that could represent familiar sounds, for example, the Rain Maker (useful for water sounds), wind instruments, a Guiro, small bells, drums, woodblocks, beaters. Ask the children to experiment with different instruments to see which sounds correspond best to the sounds heard in the school grounds.

Follow-up
Using your collection of instruments let the children explore the differences and sort them into three sets: banged, blown and strummed. Ask them to feel the vibrations of the instruments as they are played.

Shapely environments

Age range
Five to seven.

Group size
Individuals or small groups.

What you need
A range of tuned and untuned instruments, paper and pens.

What to do
Take the children for a walk in the grounds or in the local park. Ask them to observe the different landscapes and to draw their shapes and outlines on paper.

Back in the classroom, ask the children to use their outlines as a form of musical notation and to represent them as sounds. Encourage them to experiment with a variety of musical instruments. Accompany this activity with a discussion about form and long/short, sharp/soft and high/low sounds.

Follow-up
The children might like to share their shapes and patterns with friends. They could also ask the friends to 'play' the outlines on instruments of their choice.

Environmental graphic scores

Age range
Five to eleven.

Group size
Small groups or individuals.

What you need
A range of tuned and untuned instruments, sugar paper, felt-tipped pens, adhesive, a collection of small natural objects (pebbles, feathers, conkers, acorns, etc.).

What to do
Take the children for a walk in the school grounds or in a nearby park. Ask them to listen to all the different noises they can hear: children playing, birds, cars, lorries, rain, wind and so on.

Then ask them to think what graphic shape would best represent each sound. The children might like to experiment with a variety of lines, squiggles and dots (see illustration). While outdoors, they should also collect some pebbles, feathers and other small objects to decorate their 'environmental scores'.

Back in the classroom, the children can try various musical instruments to see if they can 'play' their scores. They could also try 'playing' a friend's score.

Follow-up
Create a display of the children's environmental graphic scores.

PE/Dance

Follow-my-leader

Age range
Five upwards.

Group size
The whole class.

What you need
No special requirements.

What to do
Follow-my-leader is a good warm-up activity that can accommodate all sorts of features in the school grounds. If your playground is marked out with netball or rounders lines, for example, you could lead the children jogging along the lines, moving crisply into 90° angles before turning. Alternatively, the teacher or a pupil could call out directions for pupils to turn left, right or go forwards.

Rounders bases can be used to create obstacles for weaving in and out of, to give greater variety to commands, for example, 'Touch red base, jump up and down'.

Follow-up
Other leadership games can also be played in the playground. Here are some examples: Simple Simon Says in which only commands prefaced by the words 'Simple Simon Says' are to be obeyed; Trust Walk in which one child is blindfolded and another leads him or her through a series of obstacles such as rounders bases, either by holding his or her hand or by calling out instructions.

Hand dancing

Age range
Five to nine.

Group size
Pairs and individuals.

What you need
Bags, trays, egg-boxes and any other suitable collecting equipment; a tape-recorder and a recording of gentle music; old gloves, make up, paint.

What to do
The purpose of this activity is to get the children to study the detailed outlines of natural objects and to create hand dances using them as a stimulus.

First take the children on a sensory walk in the school grounds as described on page 10. Ask them to bring back conkers, pebbles, feathers, leaves and such like. The children should then have time to study the shapes of their objects and to select one which has an outline they like. Working alone to begin with, they should trace the outline with their hands, first on the ground and then in the air. They should be as precise as possible until they can recall the outline without looking at the object. This part of the activity could be accompanied by music to help the children concentrate.

The children should then choose partners, sit on the floor facing each other and practise mirroring each other's outlines until they know both sequences. To enliven their performances of hand dances they might like to decorate their hands or a pair of old gloves with make up or paint.

Let the children check their objects for detail to make their hand dances as accurate as possible.

Follow-up
Make the whole action bigger so that the entire body is involved in the movements, and must travel from the spot. The children could try to use other parts of the body instead of the hands, thereby creating more interesting movements to build a dance sequence.

Land work

Age range
Nine to eleven.

Group size
The whole class, pairs or individuals.

What you need
Selected rhythmic accompaniment.

What to do
This activity focuses on performing a dance based on the work associated with the school environment. Start by teaching the children the country dance 'Strip the Willow', explaining how it is based on the actions of stripping bark from willow branches for basket-making.

'Strip the Willow' is a simple country dance. Its parts can form a basis for other dances.

The top couple performs the dance and finishes at the bottom of the set. The dance continues with couple no. 2 performing the sequence, then the other couples in turn until couple no. 1 becomes the top couple again.

Bars 1–4	Couple no. 1 swings with each other with left arms linked.
4–16	Girl no. 1 swings with boy no. 2 (right arm), then with her partner (left arm), boy no. 3 (right arm), partner (left arm), boy no. 4 (right).
16–20	Couple no. 1 swings with crossed wrists (clockwise) at the bottom of the set.
20–32	Couple no. 1 progresses up the set by boy swinging alternatively with girls 4, 3, 2 (right arms) and partner (left).
32–36	Couple no. 1 swings clockwise with crossed wrists at top of set.
36–48	Couple no. 1 progresses down the set performing the same swinging pattern as before, but now at the same time as each other to meet at the bottom of the set (see illustration).

Ask the children to think of work which could be the theme of the dance, for example, marking out lines for games, weeding, mowing, planting or even picking up litter.

Choose a few ideas and lead the class in individual improvisation miming these actions. Then allow each pupil to create his or her own short sequence. Develop this as a rhythmic sequence with a specific number of counts, for example, sixteen. Mention work songs and rail gangs, choosing a suitable piece of music with a clear rhythm.

After each sixteen counts, travel using improvised or taught step patterns (for example, galloping, skipping, side-steps) for the next sixteen counts. Continue by repeating the actions and the travelling.

Follow-up

● Ask the children to meet someone after sixteen travel counts and perform the actions for them in a 'question and answer' style, then continue with the travelling to meet someone else.
● You might also like to make a whole class dance grouping the pupils according to their activity.
● This activity could be pursued in conjunction with 'Walking the bounds' on page 13.

All around us

Age range
Nine to eleven.

Group size
Pairs or individuals.

What you need
Paper, pencils.

What to do
This activity is about creating movement based on shapes and patterns observed in the environment.

Take the children for a walk in the school grounds, asking them to choose three shapes or patterns in the environment which they find particularly interesting. For younger children, you might want to combine this activity with 'Identifying shapes and angles' on page 21. The children may want to draw the shapes during their walk.

Ask the children to observe lines of pitches, goal-posts, huts, bricks, fences, trees, circles of flowers, wall markings, stones, leaves, swinging ropes, gates, branches.

They should then make up a body shape or a short action to show each one of the chosen shapes or patterns. Avoid over-using hands and arms — there are other body parts which could make the movements more imaginative. Join these movements together, perhaps using some linking actions to make the sequence flow.

Can the class guess which objects inspired the sequence?

Follow-up
Working in pairs, the children could teach each other their sequences to build up a short dance. They should try to show the differences in speed, level and energy between the different parts of the dance.

Tracking and trailing 1

Age range
Seven to nine.

Group size
The whole class, pairs or individuals.

What you need
Bark, conkers, moss, pebbles, feathers and similar small objects found outdoors.

What to do
This activity is designed to explore natural textures through dance and language.

Take the children for a walk in the school grounds and ask them to collect objects with an interesting texture such as moss, bark or conkers. You may need to explain to them that they are not expected to bring back litter.

Younger children may need help with communicating the tactile qualities of their objects. Ask them to find words which describe what their object feels like and what it does, for example, bobbly, scratchy bark or a tickly, soft feather.

Select a few words and ask the children to improvise movements in quick response. Explore different ways of saying these words.

Allow the children to explore the qualities of their own objects and ask them to make up a short sequence showing different speeds, levels and directions.

Follow-up
Explore the use of speech with movement by saying or chanting the action words/object names in a way which complements the movement.

Tracking and trailing 2

Age range
Seven to eleven.

Group size
The whole class, pairs or individuals.

What you need
Pencils and paper.

What to do
The purpose of this task is to let the children discover for themselves the pathways in and around the school and to use them as a stimulus for a 'travel dance'.

Take the children for a walk in the school grounds and ask them to find as many paths as possible in the school grounds, mapping them out in rough. The resulting map will show a criss-cross of straight and curved lines, circles and zigzags. Look for animal tracks and man-made roads, paths and short-cuts.

Return to the hall and ask the children to choose one of their observed pathways, working in pairs. Then ask them to recreate as many ways of travelling down their chosen pathway as possible, for example, running, stepping, hopping, sliding, creeping.

You could challenge the children further by asking them to show what kind of creature uses the pathway in the way they move. The pairs could also try to devise more imaginative ways of travel by supporting, pulling, pushing or balancing each other.

The pathways could be enlarged or reduced in scale according to the amount of space available.

Follow-up
● The whole class could recreate a chosen route by building the environment using bodies, emphasising shapes and levels while others travel through the trail.
● You might like to pursue this activity in conjunction with the activities in the 'Journeys' chapter (see pages 102–107).

Drama

All the fun of the fair

Age range
Seven to eleven.

Group size
The whole class.

What you need
Dressing-up clothes, hoops, balls, baskets, flowers, bean bags, mini-stilts.

What to do
Ask the children if they have ever been to a fair. Talk about what fairs are like nowadays. Then tell them what it was like hundreds of years ago. Explain how different tradesmen and peddlers would come from far away to sell their wares and how entertainers, jugglers, fortune-tellers and the like would also gather around.

Together with the children, make a list of the sort of characters who might come to a fair. Give them examples such as the following: a pedlar selling ribbons, laces, buttons, theads, needles and wool; a child sent to market with lambs to sell; a travelling cobbler; a pie-seller; a crystal-ball gazer; a woman selling home-made sweets; shepherds and cowherds looking for work; farmers selling their vegetables. Talk about the sort of cries or patter they would use to attract customers.

Now ask the children to invent their own characters who will go to a fair in the playground. Ask them to think about the age of the characters, where they might have come from, how they might walk, what they would wear and so on. Would they have come to buy or to

sell? How important is the fair to them? Ask them to practise walking about in role before you stage a fair in the playground.

Follow-up
● You could use this role-play with some of the other activities such as 'Walking the bounds' on page 13 or 'Stripping the Willow' on page 81.
● Set up a pageant or a promenade performance for other classes.

Theatre in the round

Age range
Seven to eleven.

Group size
The whole class working in small groups.

What you need
Chalk.

What to do
Ask the children what they know about theatre buildings. Have they ever been inside one? Draw a plan showing the stage, curtains and the tiered seating areas. Then explain that the first theatres were open-air structures like the Greek amphitheatres. If possible show them a diagram of an amphitheatre.

Take the children into a grassy part of the grounds and ask them to sit in a circle. You might be able to take advantage of a natural feature in your school grounds – a natural dip in the ground which can be in the centre of the performing area, for example. Discuss what actors might do so that the entire audience can see and hear the story – walking around the circle, turning, repeating lines and actions. Practise these with simple lines and actions like a knock-knock joke until everyone has got the idea.

Now read out a simple version of a myth or legend, perhaps the story of King Midas. Ask the children to divide into groups and practise acting out the story. You will need to help each group with casting, as well as with breaking down the story into manageable chunks. During their practice, ask the children to think about

performing for an amphitheatre audience. It might help to draw a large circle on the ground for each group.

When they have had plenty of opportunities to practise and perfect their story, ask each group to perform it in the improvised amphitheatre.

The ancient Greeks used comic and tragic masks for their performances. The children might like to cut out and paint their own masks.

Follow-up
● You could build up your own pageant of myths for performance to the whole school. This might form a part of a larger unit of work on the ancient world, myths and fables.
● You could also invite a theatre-in-education company to perform in your school grounds.

Centre of attention

Age range
Seven to eleven.

Group size
The whole class working in groups of four to seven.

What you need
Concentric circles painted or chalked on the ground.

What to do
All children understand that the key to drama is pretending to be someone else. They do not necessarily feel able to do this outside the context of spontaneous play unless they are given support. One of the most important drama activities is, therefore, character-building.

You might like to start with a character from a story you have been reading, particularly if you are working with younger children. Older children might prefer to make up their own characters. In either case, you should first agree with the group the basic facts about the character – name, age, gender and so on. If they are using a character from a story, you should establish that everyone knows what the character did in the story. If they are making up their own character, they should agree what he or she did in the last twenty-four hours, for example, went to school, robbed a bank or broke her leg.

Ask each group to present their character to the class. To prepare their presentation, one group member should take on the role of the character, while the others play important people in the character's life – family members, friends, enemies, teachers, employers.

For the presentation, the whole group should stand in the concentric circles with the main character at the centre. The distance of group members from the centre should show how closely involved they are with the character. If the character were Cinderella, for example, the first circle would surely contain the Fairy Godmother; the last circle might contain one of the servants at the ball.

When everyone is in position, each group member should speak one sentence which describes what they have noticed about the character or how they feel about her or him. Then the character at the centre should speak a sentence, describing his or her feelings about the others.

Follow-up
Children could try swapping places in the centre of attention in a well-known story. What if the Giant were at the centre of the story of Jack and the Beanstalk, for example? They might like to explore stories in this way and then to re-write them.

Religious education

The Christmas story

Age range

Five upwards.

Group size

Up to the whole class.

What you need

Materials to build a stable and a crib in your school grounds, for example, plastic sheeting, partition screens, fencing posts, a large box, straw, a doll to represent Jesus.

What to do

Although most British children are relatively familiar with the Christmas story, many are uncertain of the details. Building a crib and staging a Christmas journey in the school grounds can bring this home to them.

Read a version of the story to the children. Then ask them where in the school grounds they would like to build the manger.

Depending on the size of your group, choose how much of the story you would like to enact. You could show Mary and Joseph looking for accommodation and finally being offered the stable, the journey of the three kings, the journey of the shepherds, or all of these.

Together with the children, divide the journey into stages, marked by conversations between the characters or characters and passers-by. Script some dialogue, explaining to the children that they are free to elaborate it. Cast the children, making sure that everyone interested has a role to play. There are plenty of characters to choose from, apart from the leads — angels, shepherds, innkeepers, Herod's courtiers.

One of the messages of the Nativity story is that among those who came to see Jesus were the rich and the poor, as well as representatives of different countries. Ask the children if they would like to add other characters to make the journey. Who would they be? What gifts would they bring?

Follow-up

● You could use the stable as a site for an outdoor carol service.
● Other religious stories can also be visualised in this concrete way.

Rangoli patterns

Age range

Five upwards.

What you need

Nailboards or geoboards (available as a maths resource in many schools), elastic bands, card, crayons and markers, white and coloured chalk, metre rulers.

What to do

Tell the children about the Hindu festival of Diwali which occurs at the end of October. It celebrates the god Vishnu and his wife Lakshmi and their incarnation as human beings. During Diwali, Hindus paint geometrical patterns on the floors, and inner and outer walls of their houses.

Show the children how they can create a variety of Rangoli patterns using nailboards with four or five pins and elastic bands.

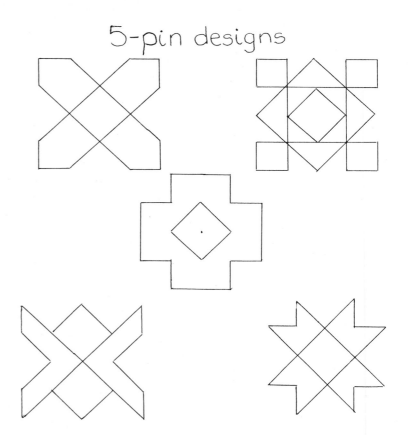

5-pin designs

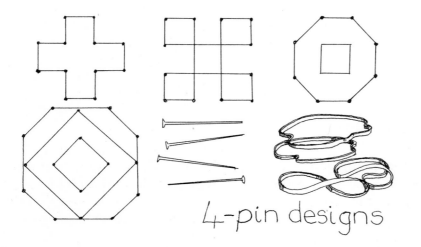

4-pin designs

Older children might like to transfer the patterns on to the playground by measuring distances between the pins, multiplying them to get a good-sized transfer and chalking the enlarged patterns on the tarmac. The patterns can then be filled in with coloured chalk.

Follow-up

Hindus often exchange Diwali cards. The children might like to design their own cards and make them into a wall display. A simple way of transferring their designs on to card is to mark the top of each pin on the nailboard and press the card against it.

An Eid picnic

Age range
Five upwards.

Group size
The whole class.

What you need
Picnic food and drink, henna powder, lemon juice, small yoghurt pots, matchsticks or cocktail sticks, water.

What to do
At the end of the month of fasting called Ramadan, Muslims celebrate breaking of the fast with the festival of Eid-ul-Fitr. They prepare elaborate meals, visit relatives and friends and give sweets and presents to children in the family.

Find out when the Eid falls this year and the next and explain to the children the idea of a movable feast and the lunar calendar, according to which the Muslim calendar is organised. Tell the children how it compares with the Gregorian calendar used by the Western Christians.

Prepare a picnic in the school grounds to celebrate Eid. The children might like to paint their hands with Mendhi patterns, which the Asian Muslims have traditionally done to celebrate special occasions (see illustration). You will need to write to parents to obtain their permission, since the patterns are painted using henna and take some time to wash off.

To make the Mendhi mixture, put a few spoonfuls of henna powder into a yoghurt pot. Add a little lemon juice and warm water and mix thoroughly. Apply the mixture in swirling patterns to the palm of the hand with a matchstick or a cocktail stick. Leave it on for about fifteen minutes, then wash off with warm water.

You will need to apply the mixture yourself or get helpers, parents or older children to assist you.

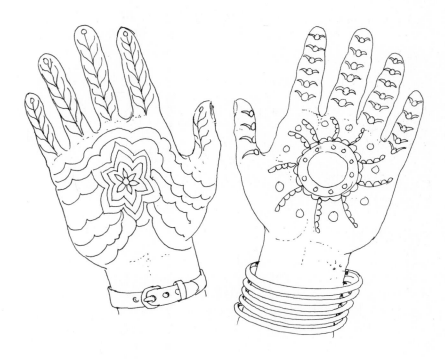

Follow-up
The month of Ramadan reminds Muslims what it is like to be hungry and that they should help the poor and the hungry in other parts of the world. Talk to the children about the work charities do and see if they would like to be involved in raising money for a charity of their choice.

Holy water

Age range
Seven to nine.

Group size
The whole class or small groups.

What you need
To suggest the crossing of a great river, you could use one of the following: drawing a river on the playground; laying out a length of old stair carpet; making use of a natural feature of the school grounds such as a winding path; assembling a line of children two or more deep, making waving motions with their arms or with streamers; using a length of cloth held up at each end by two children.

What to do
Talk to the children about the importance of water in sustaining life on earth. What happens in countries suffering from long droughts? Mention the dangers of water such as floods and sea storms.

Take the children for a walk in the school grounds after the rain. Ask them to look at changes that the rain has made. Do the grounds look cleaner? Are there any puddles? What about the raindrops — are there any decorating cobwebs or cables?

Talk to the children about the literal and symbolic uses of water in most religions. All the major religions tell stories of miraculous journeys across water to safety or to a new life, and the story of the crossing of the Red Sea, taken from the Old Testament, is one of them. Tell the children the following simplified version of the story.

The Crossing of the Red Sea
The Israelites were living in Egypt. They were treated like slaves, beaten and killed by the Pharaoh. Moses, who was their leader, could speak to God. He asked God to help them. God agreed.

For a long time the Pharaoh refused to let the Israelites go but God sent punishments. Plagues of insects called locusts came to Egypt and ate up all the crops. The Pharaoh still refused to let them go. Finally, the firstborn son in every Egyptian family was found dead. The Pharaoh agreed.

The Israelites set off as quickly as possible. They rode into the desert on their camels. Then the Pharaoh changed his mind. He sent his army after them.

Soon the Pharaoh's army was only just behind them. The Red Sea was just ahead of them. They were trapped. The people blamed Moses. 'We should have stayed in Egypt,' they said.

So Moses spoke to God again. God told Moses what to do. He raised his staff and stretched it out in front of him. The water rolled back on both sides, like curtains, and the Israelites rode across the riverbed.

When the Pharaoh's army saw this, they followed the Israelites but the water rolled back and washed them away. The Israelites were saved.

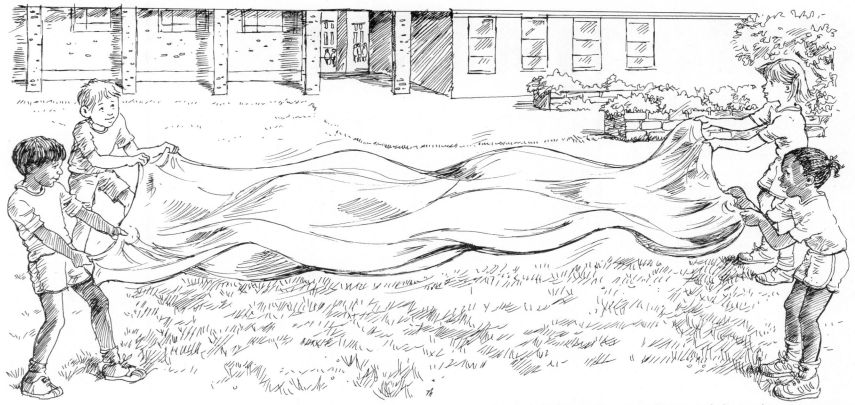

Such stories are an important means of grasping religious truths and they have traditionally been enacted by the believers. Tell the children that they will be enacting the story they have just heard. Ask them to choose the narrator, Moses and the Pharaoh, and divide the rest of the class into groups. Break up the preliminary events of the story into scenes and rehearse them. Then rehearse the central event of the story, the sea crossing. The children could make hissing, whooshing noises for the wind that parts the Red Sea. They could lie down, link hands or make arches with their arms to make a bridge of bodies.

When the children have rehearsed their dramatisation, they might like to perform it in the school grounds or indoors for the whole school.

Follow-up

● Tell the children other miraculous stories involving water such as the Muslim story of the Well of Ishmael or the Hindu story of Rama's rescue of Sita from the island of Lanka.
● Describe the use of water in baptism in various Christian religions and by the Sikhs.
● Discuss the image of crossing the river as a way of describing the cycle of life and death.

Celebrations

Many of our religious and cultural festivals are traditionally celebrated outside, as well as indoors. You might like to make a calendar of celebrations for your school, each of which could serve as a focus for a variety of themes. Activities in this chapter refer to both religious and secular celebrations, but you will find other activities, celebrating religious festivals in 'Religious Education', pages 90–95.

Fire festivals

Bonfire night

Age range
Five upwards.

Group size
The whole class.

What you need
Fuel for the bonfire (check school regulations); old newspapers, old clothes and a cardboard mask for the guy; paints, glitter, card and glue for the paintings.

What to do
Before you start this activity, check with your headteacher where in the grounds you can have a bonfire. You might also like to consult the school's landlord.

Bonfire night, celebrated on 5 November, commemorates the foiling of Guy Fawkes' plot to blow up the Houses of Parliament. This is a historical event which the children should be able to retell within the terms of the National Curriculum.

Prepare your bonfire in a convenient spot in the school grounds. The guy can be made very simply by stuffing old clothes with crumpled newspaper.

Although burning the guy is a well-established custom, some teachers may not want to encourage the burning of a human effigy. They could focus instead on recalling the details of the gunpowder plot. Rather than

burning the guy, the children could chant the following traditional rhyme around the bonfire:

> Remember, remember
> The fifth of November
> Gunpowder, treason and plot.
> I see not reason
> Why Guy Fawkes' treason
> Should ever be forgot.

Follow-up
- The children could find out more about the Houses of Parliament and about democracy. Are there any countries which do not have a parliament? How are they governed?
- What are the peaceful uses of gunpowder?
- Invite the local fire brigade and act out with them a fire in the school.

Holi

Age range

Five upwards.

What you need

Fuel for the bonfire (check appropriate safety regulations), coconuts, old clothes, food colouring or non-toxic water-soluble paint, washing-up liquid bottles, large pieces of sugar paper.

What to do

Before you start this activity, you will need to check with your headteacher where in the school grounds you could have a bonfire. You may also want to contact the school's landlord.

Tell the children about the Hindu festival of Holi which falls between February and March. It celebrates the story of Prahlad, son of the demon king, who refused to worship his father. The angry father ordered him to be burnt alive, but because Prahlad thought only of God, he was saved. The Holi celebrations begin with lighting a bonfire on the eve of the festival. The following day people eat food such as coconuts that have been roasted in the Holi fire. Barriers of caste and rank are forgotten, and people chase each other down the street and throw coloured water and powder at each other.

Ask the children to fill the washing-up liquid bottles with coloured water and to change into old clothes. Prepare your bonfire and, if possible, put some coconuts in to roast. The children can squirt coloured water at each other while the bonfire is burning.

If this seems too unruly, or if the weather does not suit an outdoor activity, you can ask the children to make Holi pictures by fixing sugar paper to the walls and squirting paint at it. They might try to recreate the flames of a bonfire.

Follow-up

● Ask the children to find out about uses of fire. What other forms of energy do we use? Do any of them require fire in their production?
● What happens to wood that was burned in the fire? Can fire burn without air?

New beginnings

The Chinese New Year

Age range
Five upwards.

Group size
The whole class.

What you need
Card, glue, glitter, elastic bands, paint, a stapler, lengths of dowelling, ribbon, string, curtain rings, bin liners, scissors or scalpel.

What to do
The Chinese New Year celebrations include street dances in which people wearing lion and dragon masks make as much noise as possible. The story behind this custom goes as follows: villages along the Yellow River endured periodic attacks of a monster who destroyed their homes and crops. After a while, the villagers discovered that the monster was frightened of loud noises, bright lights and the colour red, so they started dancing, shouting, wearing bright-coloured masks and putting up paper lanterns to keep him away.

Show the children how to make a range of decorations on the Chinese New Year theme. To make simple paper lanterns, the children should cut slits in a card rectangle and staple or glue it so as to make a

Chinese paper lantern

cut slits

stick ends together

push middle outwards

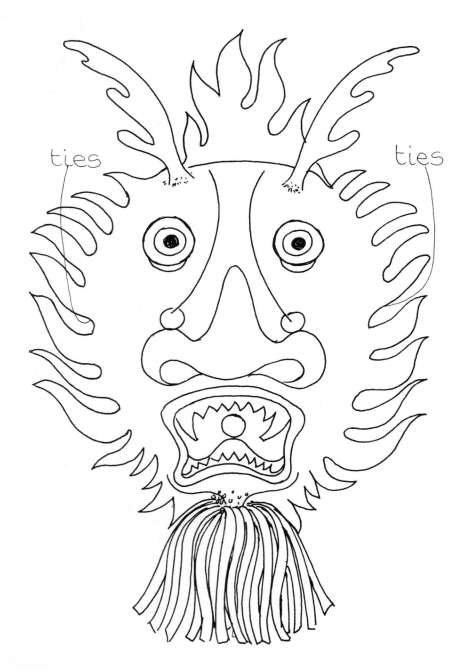

ties   ties

cylinder. The slats can then be pushed outwards to create the lantern effect. The children could paint their lanterns and decorate them with glitter. For younger children, the slits would have to be cut in advance.

The children can design their own dragon masks, but the Chinese ones usually have a long streaming mane which can be made from strips of paper or ribbons (see illustration). They can either wear their masks, held in place with elastic bands or ribbon, or fix them to a length of dowelling and hold them aloft as part of a dragon dance.

The Chinese also celebrate the New Year with kite flying. The children could make their own kites (see page 42).

You might like to explain to the children the twelve-yearly cycle of the Chinese horoscope. There are many stories about its origin; the most common one tells how the Emperor of China invited all the people and animals to a feast but only twelve turned up: a rat, an ox, a tiger, a rabbit, a dragon, a serpent, a horse, a ram, a monkey, a rooster, a dog and a pig. The emperor was so pleased to see them that he named a year after each one. The children could make costumes for the different animals or mime whichever animal they like.

Follow-up

● Talk to the children about the cycle of the year and about lunar and calendar months. Explain that the Chinese year lasts thirteen lunar months. Do they know of other calendars, for example, the Muslim or the Hindu one?
● Ask them to find out when the Muslims, the Jews, the Hindus and the Russian Orthodox believers would celebrate their New Year and what their celebrations would be like.

Easter

Age range
Five upwards.

Group size
The whole class.

What you need
Hen's eggs, pins, beakers, paint, paintbrushes, card, paper doilies, tissue paper, pipe-cleaners, adhesive, scissors, spoons, ping-pong balls, small chocolate eggs.

What to do
Easter is a Christian festival with roots in earlier religions. For Christians it is the time of Christ's crucifixion and resurrection. Palm Sunday, when Christ rode into Jerusalem on a donkey, is observed with processions and the giving out of dried palm leaves folded into the shapes of crosses.

Easter is also celebrated in our society as a pagan festival. Its origins, as a fertility festival, are largely forgotten but they are still acknowledged by gifts of chocolate eggs. An egg hunt in the school grounds could be a lot of fun. Hide the eggs and give the children verbal or written clues. Make sure no one gets more than their fair share.

In some cultures, Easter is celebrated with blown and brightly painted hen's eggs. They are first pricked with a pin at both ends and the contents blown out into a beaker. The contents are traditionally used to make simnel cakes. The children could paint blown eggs and create a class display of Easter eggs.

Why not hold egg and spoon races in your grounds?

You may prefer to use ping-pong balls instead of eggs.

Easter is also associated with parades in which people wear elaborate hats and head-dresses. Ask the children to design their own Easter bonnets and hold an Easter Parade in the school grounds. Paper doilies stuck to circles of card make a good base for the hat. Paper flowers made from coloured crêpe or tissue paper and pipe-cleaners can then be added.

Follow-up
Both the Christian and the pre-Christian festivals are celebrations of life. Talk to the children about the processes of reproduction. What creatures are not born from eggs? How do trees and plants reproduce?

Take a walk in the school grounds and identify the signs of new life: trees budding, insects' eggs, seeds beginning to germinate. Perhaps you could start a bulb-planting programme.

Invite mothers and fathers with small babies into school. Get the children to look at the differences between babies and children and the milestones of development.

Journeys

A journey through the school grounds helps the children see the school as a series of different environments rather than a static location. Your journeys can be imaginative, involving drama and role-play, or technical, involving orienteering skills.

Other activities involving journeys can be used in conjunction with this section. You could try 'A guided tour', page 15, 'The Christmas story', page 91, 'Serial vision', page 72, 'Follow-my-leader', page 79 and 'Tracking and trailing', page 84.

Great escapes

Hansel and Gretel

Age range
Five to nine.

Group size
Pairs.

What you need
Chalk, white bread.

What to do
Tell the children the story of Hansel and Gretel. They were two children taken to the middle of the forest and abandoned by their stepmother and father. Twice they found their way back by following the trail of white stones that Hansel had left. The third time Hansel had no stones so he used pieces of bread instead. The birds ate the bread and when Hansel and Gretel set off for home there was no trail to guide them. They ended up in the clutches of the witch who lived in the Gingerbread House and from whom they finally managed to escape.

Give each pair of children a collection of white stones. These can be pieces of chalk. Tell them to set off on a journey in the school grounds and to leave a trail of stones behind them. After five or ten minutes they should retrace their steps, picking up their trail. Alternatively, tell one child to set off on a journey leaving a trail. After five minutes, the other child should go in search of her partner.

They can also lay a trail of bread pieces and leave them for twenty-four hours. Are they still there the next day? What has happened to the missing ones?

Follow-up
Talk about other ways used in the past to mark out roads: standing-stones, milestones, signposts, hedges, cat's eyes. What about sea lanes? How do aeroplane and submarine pilots find their way about?

Through the labyrinth

Age range
Five upwards.

Group size
Pairs.

What you need
Chalk, lengths of string or wool.

What to do
Tell the children the story of Theseus and the Minotaur. Theseus was sent into the labyrinth to kill the Minotaur, half-bull and half-man, or be killed. However, he was helped by Ariadne, the daughter of King Minos. She gave him a ball of string which he unrolled as he went through the labyrinth in search of the monster. After he had killed it, he was able to find his way out again by rolling the string back up into a ball.

Give a ball of string to each pair of children. One child holds the end while the partner makes a journey through the grounds and/or the building, unravelling the wool at the same time. When the ball is completely unravelled, the journeying child rolls the string back up to return to her partner. Alternatively, the child holding the end can now retrace the journey to find his partner.

Follow-up
If your school has a field, you can build a turf maze. Ask the children to design it first; they could draw a number of possible shapes to see which is most pleasing and most practical. This can involve some work on symmetry.

To build the maze you will need to dig small earth ramps for the walls and cover them with turf. This is heavy work but one school persuaded their local army unit to do the digging for them.

Journeys of discovery

A treasure hunt

Age range
Five to eleven.

Group size
Smal groups or pairs.

What you need
Enough compasses to give one to each pair or group, small prizes for each pair or group.

What to do
Hide 'treasure tokens' in different locations in the grounds. The tokens can be pieces of paper, cardboard or plastic, but each should be distinctly numbered. Set up a number of different orienteering points in the school grounds. These can be very simple, for example, marks on the school playground made with coloured chalk, rounders bases, existing features of the school grounds. Prepare maps for each pair or group, using simple compass directions and the orienteering points such as 'Walk north-east until you come to a red circle'. Ask them to find their treasure tokens using the maps. Tokens can then be redeemed for prizes.

Follow-up
● Make contact with local groups of Orienteers, Ramblers or Mountaineers. Ask an expert, for example, someone from the Youth Hostel Association, to visit the

school to talk to the children.
● Make a series of Treasure Hunt packs as school resources. You could incorporate seasonal factors, for example, flowers or trees in blossom, and make different packs for each season.

Hidden trails

Age range
Seven to eleven.

Group size
Pairs or individuals.

What you need
Pencils and paper.

What to do
Ask the children to design a series of hidden trails round the school. Explain that these are journeys across the school grounds that people would not take just to get from one place to another.

There could be many different kinds. Here are some examples: a trail of creepy places, a sunny walk, a trail of slimy places, a trail you can take without stepping on any cracks, a trail you can take without stepping on the

ground, a trail you can take and always be able to touch wood.

The children should begin by going out and finding their trails. Then they need to note down all the places they want to include in their trails and draw a map to show them.

Ask them to look at the signs and symbols used on maps for things like golf courses, churches, pubs and so on. They could design their own set of symbols for their trails and draw them on their maps. Perhaps they could paint or draw the symbols on the ground to mark out their trails permanently.

Follow-up

Ask the children to draw a map of their journey to school. What are the special features of their journey that they would like to include on the map?

Surveying the grounds

Surveying the grounds as a curriculum activity

Age range

This activity can be adapted for children of all ages. Older children will be able to undertake more complex survey, design and construction work. But even young children will have opinions and be capable of helping with design work.

Organisation of project

School grounds are all different, as are each school's staffing structures, timetables and approaches to teaching. Improving school grounds can take a few weeks or a lifetime. However, certain principles and processes are common to many successful schemes. These can be adapted to provide a package of work which would, ideally, form the focus of a week of suspended timetable activities or the theme for a number of curriculum activities throughout a term or year. Alternatively, they can be applied to a smaller-scale school grounds improvement.

Curriculum areas

This package of work could be adapted to form part of schemes of work in the Programmes of Study of all of the core and foundation subjects and all of the cross-curricular themes which make up the National Curriculum. Certainly a project such as this is bound to include elements of technology, maths, science, art and geography. There are also obvious opportunities for extra-curricular work and for activities spilling over into the informal curriculum.

Group size

A variety of group sizes will be required, including whole classes, groups, pairs and individuals working on their own.

What you need

You will need access to some or all of the following: old maps and photographs of the school, an up-to-date site plan, local climatic data, weather-recording equipment, measuring equipment, large sheets of paper, crayons and paint, model-making equipment (clay, cardboard, chicken wire, plaster of Paris, etc.), photocopies of survey sheets on pages 115–124, a camera, photographs of other schools and their grounds, reference books, a landscape architect or community designer, parents and other adult helpers. This is not a conclusive list!

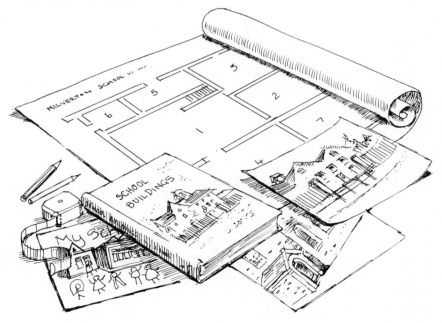

What to do

The following processes can be adapted to suit the needs of individual schools undertaking grounds improvements.

Stage 1: investigating the past

Before you start, it is worth finding out as much as you can about the history of your site. Get hold of old Ordnance Survey maps of the school. Assemble as many old photographs as you can. This can be achieved by asking the children whose parents or grandparents went to the school to contribute and by asking local residents to help. A visit to the local library may reveal old newspaper articles. Taped interviews with local residents may yield surprising information about how the site has developed. Things to look for include parish boundary walls or hedges, indications of former land use and old photographs. All of this provides a fascinating context in which to set the project.

Stage 2: initial site appraisal

In most schools, children, staff, parents and the local community all have strong opinions about the school's site. It helps to allow people to voice them in a variety of different ways while the agenda is still open. Children and adults alike are often very conservative and you will need to find a delicate balance between allowing free opinion-gathering sessions and giving an input which is creative and challenging without being prescriptive.

Children
Ask the children to:
● take you to their favourite and least favourite places in the grounds;
● draw a map of the grounds showing where they like to go and what they like to do there;
● contribute to a brainstorming session in which you

focus on 'likes' and 'dislikes';
● talk to you individually and in groups of friends about their views of the grounds;
These activities are appropriate for developing skills in English, art, personal and social education and environmental education.

Staff
Ask all the teaching and non-teaching staff their opinion and produce an annotated school map or comment bank. Display it in the staff room. You may want to ask for specific comments on the local climate (and microclimate within the grounds, such as windy spots), on major land shapes within the site, on buildings and on the boundaries and approaches to the school. Ask them to think what lessons they could teach in the school grounds.

At this stage it is also important to find out who is responsible for maintaining your grounds. They will be able to provide maps and other advice. Under the Local

Government and Education Acts of 1988 new
regulations were introduced which may affect this area
of activity.

Parents and local community
Get a clear idea of their views and keep them closely
informed about the exciting project you are about to
undertake. There are many different ways of canvassing
opinion, from questionnaire to a parents' evening or
public meeting. You may wish to start this process now
or wait until the next stage.

Stage 3: site analysis

Various kinds of mapping and survey work are required
to give you the more detailed information base from
which you can feel confident to initiate change.

Depending on the age of your children the survey on
pages 108–113 may be a useful way of opening
everyone's eyes to exactly what is on your site. The
whole survey can be adapted or you may want to look
at one section of it at any one time, to fit in with a
particular subject or project.

The act of placing your school in a context is full of
geography, history and environmental education.
Measuring, recording and handling data involves a
variety of mathematical skills. Identifying species is a
part of science. Asking and answering questions
develops vital communication skills. Critical study of the
external environment is an essential prerequisite of
environmental education or citizenship.

The survey is organised into sections which you might
want to link with specific study topics, for example, a
study of the buildings in your area or the uses of trees.
Occasionally, in order to complete a section, you will
need to teach new skills such as data collection or
species identification.

In many places it will be necessary to debate the issues raised by the act of choosing to survey something at all. Sections to do with recycling or bird habitat are obvious examples. It is hoped that the act of surveying will allow you to talk about the nature of change; how you need to know what you have and what you might have before being really equipped to consider implementing changes.

There are many other possible activities you could try. Here are a few of these, some aimed at children, some at adults, some at both:

● Ask other staff to think back to their own childhood and make a list of all the places they enjoyed. You will get answers that include tree houses, rubbish dumps, odd nooks and crannies! See how many of these you have in your grounds. This is a good way of helping yourself and other staff decide what questions to ask the children.

● Ask the children to devise a questionnaire for use with other children in the school. Questions can usefully be asked about the following: what they do at break times; what games they play and where; whether they think any areas are dangerous; whether they think any bullying takes place and, if so, by whom and where; where they go when it is cold, hot, wet or windy; whether there are enough seats and where they like sitting; what they would like to do but cannot. Whenever possible, it helps to allow these kinds of questions to come from the children.

● Ask the children to interview each other and adults connected with the site whose views they think might be of importance to them. (The caretaker and lunch-time supervisors are key people here.) Invite the adults into the classroom to discuss the problems they have spotted.

● Ask the children to produce their own annotated site plan for the grounds. If possible, give them the opportunity to create three-dimensional models of the site. These are particularly useful for visualising ideas at the next stage. Models need to be strong enough to be moved about during this period of planning.

● Ask the older children to write to organisations and individuals who might be able to help them.

● Ask the children and staff to observe and draw maps of where people go in the grounds. These can be used as a prompt for further discussion.

Stage 4: getting ideas
On the basis of the work already done, both the children and the adults will by now be able to articulate plenty of ideas. There are a number of ways in which you can ensure that the maximum possible learning takes place at this stage. As children may know one school environment only, try the following to broaden their experience.

● Take them to visit other schools, parks, etc.

● Show them pictures and photographs of a variety of architectural and landscape features. Use ideas in the survey on pages 108–113 to help you select the pictures.

● Get them to draw and photograph details of the grounds and then talk about what they like or dislike and why.

● If possible, invite a landscape architect or designer to work alongside the children, but not before they have started to develop their own ideas – some professionals may otherwise impose their own ideas!

● Discuss with them some of the issues which they may not have considered, and which did not emerge when surveying the school grounds. For example, if they want to see butterflies, they need to plant buddleia; if they want birds to visit, they have to provide food and shelter; if they want to paint a mural, they might like some help from an artist.

• Focus on emerging issues such as boundaries, shelter, entrances, signposting, seating, equipment and so on.

Stage 5: prioritising

By now you should have a profusion of ideas, some highly idealistic, some expensive and some impractical. During this crucial stage you will need to agree on the priorities. Some of the ideas can be costed by the children, others by you and a few will probably require outside help.

To help the children make choices, display a list of items and their costs, and ask them for their reactions. Children can be surprisingly good at ruling out some of the more extravagant ideas thrown up earlier. You could also ask the children to rate each idea on a 1–5 scale.

Stage 6: producing a master plan

Ideally, you should try to get a professionally-drawn master plan. This should incorporate as many of the children's ideas as possible. Even if this is not possible, you may want some kind of specialist advice at this stage, concerning timetable, costings and possible sources of income.

Stage 7: getting started

Depending on the time you are prepared to allocate, you might be getting the children to research, design, make and evaluate a minibeast shelter from old logs, looking at planting a copse or building a recycling centre.

Whatever your choice, such activities are full of curriculum possibilities. They will, in many cases, take you back to some of the processes you have been working through in the previous pages. You may wish to use ideas from this book or think of completely new ones of your own. Whatever your choice, you will find that landscape improvement can go hand in hand with lessons in the outdoor classroom.

The Learning Through Landscapes Trust and other national and local organisations can give you advice if you reach the stage where you are contemplating significant landscape changes.

There are health, safety, legal and financial implications in such work. These need not deter you, but they do need to be carefully investigated.

Reproducible materials

Teachers' notes: organising a school grounds survey

You may find it helpful to photocopy this page and carry it with you when you are conducting the survey.

Preparation checklist

In addition to the items of equipment listed here, this checklist will help you prepare for a complex activity in which small groups of children will undertake a number of tasks independently and where good organisation is important.

- How are you going to introduce the activity?
- Where are you going to introduce it? _____
- What is the purpose of the activity? Should this emerge during the activity or should it be explicitly stated? _____
- How much whole-group instruction will be required? _____
- Are there any new concepts contained in the work? If so, how will these be explained? _____
- Are there any items of vocabulary on the survey sheet which you need to look up before using them with the children? _____
- What equipment will you need? _____
- What equipment will the children need? _____
- Are there any safety issues involved? _____
- How will equipment be distributed and collected? _____
- Would the activity benefit from an input from another adult, for example, a specialist in the field? _____
- How will groups be organised? _____
- How will data be collected and recorded? (Some schools may wish to use a computer database.) _____
- How will data be analysed and displayed? _____
- What use will data be put to? _____

Equipment checklist

Compass ☐	Plastic bags ☐	Rainfall gauge ☐
Old Ordnance Survey map ☐	Pencils ☐	Thermometers ☐
Large-scale Ordnance Survey map ☐	Pens ☐	Ph strips ☐
	Camera ☐	Bug boxes ☐
Paper ☐	Video camera ☐	Hand lenses ☐
Card ☐	Metre rule ☐	Soil sieve ☐
Clipboard ☐	Trundle wheel ☐	Butterfly net ☐
	Large tape-measure ☐	Binoculars ☐
	Reference books ☐	

School grounds survey

Section 1: your school and its community

1. What can you see if you look along compass points from your site? (You may need to go outside with a teacher to do this.)

North _____

South _____

East _____

West _____

2. Where is your school?

In the middle of a town/city ☐

On the edge of a town/city ☐

In a village/in the country ☐

3. How far do you travel to get to school each day?

Less than 1km ☐

1–2km ☐

2–4km ☐

More than 5km ☐

4. How do you travel to school?

On foot ☐

By bicycle ☐

By bus ☐

By car ☐

Section 2: the buildings

1. When was your school built?

	Before 1918	1919-45	1945-60	1960-80	After 1980
Main buildings					
Extra buildings					

2. Walls, fences and hedges

Have you got any fences or walls which are as follows:

Material	Y/N	Length		
Brick wall				
Stone wall				
Wire-fence (chain link)				
Wire-fence (other type)				
Wooden fence				
Other (specify)				

Do you have any of the following on your walls/fences?

Painted murals ☐

Lichen ☐

Moss ☐

Other plants ☐

Other (specify) ——————————

Do the fences, walls or hedges around your school grounds keep people and/or dogs out when you want them to? Y/N

If not, what are the reasons?

We like people to come in ☐

Holes in fence etc. ☐

Gates left open ☐

Other (specify) ——————————

3. Courtyards

Have you got one? Y/N

If so, do you use it during classes? ☐   Do you use it during break? ☐

At other times? (specify) ——————————

What does it have in it? (plants, a pond etc.) ——————————

4. Other buildings

What other buildings do you have on your school site?

Greenhouse ☐   Temporary classrooms ☐

Outside toilets ☐   Other (specify) ☐

Storage sheds ☐

5. Outdoor swimming pool
Does your school have an outside swimming pool? Y/N

6. Seating
What is there for people to sit down on in the tarmac areas of your grounds?

How many people can sit on the following?

Seating	Benches	Chairs	Kerbs	Logs	Walls	Other (specify)
Brick						
Concrete						
Metal						
Plastic						
Wood						

7. Sculpture
Do you have any pieces of sculpture on your school site? Y/N

8. Litter collection and recycling
Is litter collected on your school site? Y/N

How frequently does collection occur?

(D=daily, W=weekly, T=termly, WR= when required, O=other)

Do you or other pupils use any of these and where are they?

(PF=playing field, HS=hard play area, G=garden, O=other)

Bins	Metal	Plastic	Designed by pupils	Other (specify)
Number				
Place				

Do you recycle things in your school? Y/N

If YES, which of these do you recycle?

Aluminium ☐   Clothes ☐

Paper ☐   Glass ☐

Other (specify) ──────────

9. Markings

Which of these do you have marked on your playground or walls?
Please indicate Y/N.

Basketball	☐	Compass	☐	Dragons	☐
Footprints	☐	Ladders (plain)	☐	Map (UK)	☐
Number square	☐	Ladders (numbered)	☐	Map (county)	☐
Tennis	☐	Caterpillars	☐	Rings	☐
Football	☐	Hopscotch	☐	Shadow clock	☐
Football (5-a-side)	☐	Padder tennis	☐	Shapes	☐
Stop signs	☐	Solar system	☐	Chess	☐
Cricket stumps	☐	Maze	☐	Hockey	☐
Snakes (plain)	☐	Netball	☐	Rounders	☐
Snakes (numbered)	☐	Other (specify)	☐		

10. Playground equipment

Do you have any of the following equipment for use on your school site?

Aerial runways	☐	Climbing frame (permanently fixed)	☐
Elevated walkway	☐	Slide	☐
Tunnel (concrete)	☐	Tunnel (plastic)	☐
Tunnel (metal)	☐	Climbing frame (can be moved)	☐
Monkey ladder	☐	Swings	☐
Netball hoop	☐	Adventure park	☐
Other (specify)	☐		

11. Equipment
Do you use any of these?

Balls ☐ Marbles ☐
Rackets ☐ Bats ☐
Mats ☐ Rollerskates ☐
Cones ☐ Old tyres ☐
Skipping ropes ☐ Other (specify) _____

Section 3: Grass and flower beds

1. Garden areas
Do you have any areas of garden in your school site? Y/N
Do you have any of the following?

Type	Y/N	Area
Chequer-board garden		
Ground cover		
Herbaceous border		
Rose-beds		
Seasonal bedding		
Shrubs		
Spring bulbs		
Other (specify)		

Are any of these areas planted in beds raised above ground level? Y/N
Do you have a rockery garden? Y/N

2. Mazes
Do you have a maze on your school site? Y/N If so, what is it made of? _____

3. Grass areas

Do you have areas of grass on your school site? Y/N

Which types do you have?

Types	Y/N	Size
Sports field		
Other lawns		
Meadow with flowers		

4. Seating

What facilities are there for people to sit down in your school gardens and playing fields?

Seating	Benches	Chairs	Kerbs	Logs	Walls	Other
Concrete						
Metal						
Plastic						
Wood						
Other (specify)						

5. Orchard

Do you have an orchard in your school site? Y/N

Which types of fruit tree do you grow?

Apple ☐

Apricot ☐

Cherry ☐

Pear ☐

Plum ☐

Other (specify) _____

6. Woodlands

Do you have areas of woodland on your site? Y/N

How old is your wood?

Less than 5 years ☐

6–10 years ☐

11–15 years ☐

16–20 years ☐

More than 20 years ☐

Who planted the trees? _____

Which species of trees grow in your woodland?

Ash ☐

Chestnut ☐

Rowan ☐

Beech ☐

Holly ☐

Scots pine ☐

Birch ☐

Oak ☐

Sycamore ☐

Other (specify) _____

7. Hedges

Do you have any hedges on your site? Y/N

8. Water

Do you have any of the following on your school site? Y/N

Ditch ☐   Marsh/bog ☐   Pond ☐

River ☐   Stream ☐   Other (specify) _____

Section 4: Wildlife

1. Animals and birds
Which of the following do you see and study regularly?

Type	Present (Y/N)	Frequency of study (daily/weekly/termly/sporadic)
Birds		
Insects (butterflies)		
Insects (other)		
Mammals (small)		
Mammals (large)		
Other (specify)		

2. Attracting wildlife
Which of the following features are provided on your school site?

Feature	Y/N	Number
Bird-bath		
Bird box		
Bird hide		
Bird-table		
Bat box		
Hedgehog box		
Other (specify)		

3. Studying wildlife
Which of the following do you use to study the wildlife in your school site?

Binoculars ☐   Computer ☐   Measuring stick ☐

Trundle wheel ☐   Rain gauge ☐   Stevenson's screen ☐

Video camera ☐   Nature trail ☐   Butterfly net ☐

Hand lens ☐   Measuring tape ☐   Microscopes ☐

Soil sieves ☐   Thermometer ☐   Bird hide ☐
             (outdoor)   Other (specify) ———

4. Growing plants

Do you use a cold frame for growing plants? Y/N

Do you use a greenhouse for growing plants? Y/N

Do you have any raised beds? Y/N

Section 5: Climate and pollution

1. Monitoring climate

Do you regularly monitor the weather? Y/N

Rainfall ☐

Sunshine ☐

Temperature ☐

Wind ☐

Other (specify) _____

2. Monitoring pollution

Do you regularly monitor pollution in water? Y/N

Air ☐

Rain ☐

Other (specify) _____

Have you ever taken part in a national monitoring scheme? Y/N

If so, what was the subject? _____

What information did you collect? _____

This survey is a simpler version of one being used in the United Kingdom and Europe in a long-term school monitoring project called Esso Schoolwatch, details of which can be obtained from Learning Through Landscapes.

Resources

Grant schemes

British Gas Grassroots Action Scheme: Awards Administration, Kallaway, 2 Portland Rd, Holland Park, London W11 4LA. Tel. 071 221 7883. Conservation award scheme for young people involved in greening the community. Secondary schools, community groups and conservation charities are eligible.

Colonel Sanders Environmental Awards: c/o National Coordinator, City Gate Corporate, 7 Birchin Lane, London EC3V 9BY. Tel. 071 623 2737. Awards of up to £1,000. Retrospective and ongoing projects are eligible.

English Nature School Grants Scheme: Northminster House, Peterborough PE1 1UA. Tel. 0733 340345. Ten grants per county per year. Schemes must benefit wildlife and involve children at all stages.

The Forte Community Chest/The Conservation Foundation: 1 Kensington Gore, London SW7 2AR. Tel. 071 823 8842. Awards of up to £1,000 for community-based environmental projects.

Pondwatch, c/o The Wildfowl and Wetlands Trust, Slimbridge, Glos GL2 7BT. Tel. 0453 890333. National annual competition, awards of up to £1,000 for outstanding ponds.

Shell Better Britain Campaign, Red House, Hill Lane, Great Barr, Birmingham B43 6LZ. Tel. 021 358 0744. Awards of up to £750 on a first come, first served basis. Work must be carried out by volunteers and involve community access.

This is not an exhaustive list as new schemes are introduced every year. Further details of other grant schemes are available from Learning Through Landscapes Trust, Third Floor, Southside Offices, The Law Courts, Winchester, Hants SO23 9DL. Tel. 0962 846258.

Books

The following books, available from Southgate Publishers (0363 777 575), are produced by Learning Through Landscapes.

The Outdoor Classroom: Educational Use, Landscapes Design and Management of School Grounds (1990) Department of Education and Science. Based on research by Learning Through Landscapes, it provides detailed information on potential school improvements.

The Final Report, Eileen Adams (1990). A report on the use, design and management of school grounds.

Using School Grounds as an Educational Resource, Kirsty Young (1990). Includes thirteen studies of good practice and a section on planning change.

Ecology in the National Curriculum: a Practical Guide to Using School Grounds, Rupert Booth (1990). A range of activities linked with science attainment targets.

Butterflies: a Practical Guide to their Study in School Grounds via the National Curriculum, Dr John Feltwell (1990).

Recycling in the School Grounds, Dr John Feltwell (1992).

Limited Damage, Brian Keaney (1991). A short story set in the school grounds.

Slugs, Snails and Earthworms: a Practical Guide to Their Study in School Grounds, Dr John Feltwell (1991).

Beekeeping: a Practical Guide to Beekeeping in the School Grounds, Dr John Feltwell (1991).

Wildlife in the School Environment, co-published with the Royal Society for the Protection of Birds (1992).

The Seasons in the School Grounds, Sue Rowe (1991). A folder of curriculum activities for primary school pupils.

Science in the School Grounds, Gill Thomas (1992). Published with Southgate.

Videos: *Making the Best of your School Grounds* (1991). Practical advice aimed at primary schools.

Grounds for Examination (1992). Practical advice aimed at Secondary schools.

Useful organisations

All of these organisations produce publications and provide advice.

British Trust for Conservation Volunteers
36 St Mary's Street
Wallingford
Oxon OX10 0EU
Tel. 0491 39766

Centre for Alternative Technology
Machynlleth
Powys SY20 9AZ
Tel. 0654 702460

Civic Trust
17 Carlton House Terrace
London SW1Y 5AW
Tel. 071 930 0914

Common Ground
c/o London Ecology Centre
45 Sheldon Street
London WC2 9HJ
Tel. 071 379 3109

Council for Environmental Education
School of Education
University of Reading
London Road
Reading
Berks RG1 5AQ
Tel. 0734 756061

Countryside Commission
John Dower House
Crescent Place
Cheltenham GL50 3RA
Tel. 0242 521381

Groundwork Foundation
85–87 Cornwall Street
Birmingham B3 3BY
Tel. 021 236 8565

Living Archive
Stantonbury Campus
Stantonbury, Milton Keynes
Bucks MK14 6BN
Tel. 0908 322568

National Association for Environmental Education
Wolverhampton Polytechnic
Walsall Campus
Gorway
Walsall
West Midlands WS1 3BD
Tel. 0922 31200

National Association for Urban Studies
Lewis Cohen Urban Studies Centre
Brighton Polytechnic
68 Grand Parade
Brighton BN2 2JY
Tel. 0273 673416

National Children's Play and Recreation Unit
359–361 Euston Road
London NW1 3AL
Tel. 071 383 5455

Royal Society for the Protection of Birds
The Lodge
Sandy
Beds SG19 2DL
Tel. 0767 680551

Tidy Britain Group
The Pier
Wigan
WN3 4EX
Tel. 0942 824620

The Tree Council
35 Belgrave Square
London
SW1X 8QN
Tel. 071 235 8854

WATCH/Royal Society for Nature Conservation
The Green
Witham Park
Waterside South
Lincoln LN5 7JR
Tel. 0522 544400

World Wide Fund for Nature
Panda House
Weyside Park
Godalming
Surrey GU7 1XR
Tel. 0483 426444

Acknowledgements

The Learning Through Landscape Trust would like to thank the following schools for devising and trying out ideas: Conway Infant School, Plumstead, Greenwich; Coombes Infant and Nursery School, Arborfield, Berks; Kings Copse School, Hedge End, Hants; John Stainer School, Brockley, Lewisham.

   The following organisations have given help and ideas: Hampshire County Music Service; Hampshire Science and Technology Advisory Team; Kent Environmental Educational Team; Royal Society for the Protection of Birds; South-East Regional Play Association; Surrey Dance Project.

Other Scholastic books

Bright Ideas
The *Bright Ideas* provide a wealth of resources for busy primary school teachers. There are now over forty original and informative books to choose from, providing clearly explained and illustrated ideas on topics ranging from spelling and computer activities to Christmas art and craft. Each book contains material which can be photocopied for use in the classroom.

Bright Ideas for Early Years
The *Bright Ideas for Early Years* series has been written specially for nursery and reception teachers, playgroup leaders and all those who work with 3–6 year-olds. The books provide sound practical advice in all areas of learning. The ideas and activities are easy to follow and clearly illustrated.

Teacher Timesavers
Teacher Timesavers are a unique series of books, expertly designed to save busy primary teachers hours of preparation time. With topics ranging from history and problem solving to writing, the books offer a wealth of photocopiable activity sheets that can be used over and over again. The accompanying teacher's notes explain the purpose of each activity.

Scholastic Collections
Scholastic Collections is an exciting new series for primary teachers. Containing a large proportion of specially commissioned new material, it provides a wealth of songs, poems, games and plays to fit in with particular topics.

Inspirations
Inspirations, like the *Bright Ideas*, offer activity-centered learning in combination with advice on using the activities within the framework of the National Curriculum. It is the perfect choice for teachers who want ideas for classroom activities, but who also welcome extra information on curriculum content, assessment, recording, teaching strategies and delivery.